Praise for *The Tiger and the Rabbit*

Asha Saxena, CEO and Founder of Women Data and AI Leaders, and the Best-selling Author of *The AI Factor*. "Embracing the power of the metaverse, Web3, and AI can feel like a daunting task, but *The Tiger and the Rabbit* provides a refreshing and relatable guide to navigating these emerging technologies. AI is hotter than hot, and if you don't know it, you will be left behind. Through a compelling fable, readers will gain practical insights on building a 'rabbit' team that can leverage these AI tools to drive business success."

Sebastien BORGET, The Sandbox. "As the cofounder and COO of the Sandbox, decentralized gaming virtual world and the president of the Blockchain Game Alliance, advocating for #NFTs and blockchain in games, I know the transformative power of the metaverse, Web3, and AI. *The Tiger and the Rabbit* provides a comprehensive guide to this exciting new space and offers valuable insights into how businesses can leverage these technologies for success."

Dirk Lueth, CEO Upland, Founder OMA3. "As the cofounder and co-CEO of Uplandme, Inc. and the cofounder and chairman of the Open Metaverse Alliance for Web3 (OMA3), I highly recommend this book. OMA3 and Upland are both mentioned in *The Tiger and the Rabbit* as examples of driving various initiatives to achieve interoperability. This book offers a compelling vision for the future of business and is a must-read."

Trevor Traina, CEO and Former US Ambassador. "Having founded six companies and invested in countless others, I can say with certainty that *The Tiger and the Rabbit* is a must-read for any entrepreneur or investor looking to stay ahead in today's rapidly evolving digital landscape. In fact, government officials around the world should study the book's unique approach of using a fable to illustrate practical tips on leveraging the power of the metaverse, Web3, and AI is both engaging and insightful."

Pam Moore, Founder and CEO Brand with Soul. "As one of the most influential women in Web3, I'm thrilled to see this important topic explored in *The Tiger and the Rabbit*. This book offers practical advice for harnessing the power of the metaverse, Web3, and AI and is a must for anyone in the digital age.

Darcy Donavan, CEO, Founder of StarDawgs, Film and TV Actress, Author and Producer: "As an actress and entrepreneur, I know the value of bringing creativity, passion, and innovation to every project. With *The Rabbit and the Tiger*, readers can expect a fresh perspective on how to harness the power of emerging technologies like the metaverse, Web3, and AI to drive success in business. As the #CryptoQueen, I know that you're going to highly enjoy reading this book!"

Michael Stezner, CEO and Founder, Social Media Examiner. "If you're someone who wants to not only understand the next big wave of business innovation, but also be part of the new renaissance, then read Sandy Carter's book, *The Tiger and the Rabbit*. Your next career changing opportunity is right around the corner. Let Sandy show you the way."

ChatGPT, AI Tool. "*The Tiger and the Rabbit* offers an insightful fable on harnessing the power of the Metaverse, Web3, and AI to create a nimble 'rabbit' team."

The
Tiger
and the
Rabbit

A Business Fable

The
Tiger
and the
Rabbit

Harnessing the Power of the
Metaverse, WEB3, and AI
for Business Success

Sandy Carter

WILEY

For general information on our other products and services or for technical support, please contact our Customer Care Department within the United States at (800) 762-2974, outside the United States at (317) 572-3993 or fax (317) 572-4002.

Wiley also publishes its books in a variety of electronic formats. Some content that appears in print may not be available in electronic formats. For more information about Wiley products, visit our web site at www.wiley.com.

Library of Congress Cataloging-in-Publication Data is Available:

ISBN 9781394190126 (Cloth)
ISBN 9781394190140 (ePub)
ISBN 9781394190133 (ePDF)

Cover Design: Paul McCarthy
Cover Art: AI-Generated Image Created Using Shutterstock AI

SKY10050766_071023

To my loving family, Todd, Kassie, Maria, and my mom and dad, who bought me that robot! They inspire me every day!

To the entire Unstoppable Fam, especially our team and whales who believe in digital identity!

To all the amazing Women in Web3, AI, and the metaverse and your untiring impact!

To YOU, who are exploring the future innovations!

Contents

Foreword

Cathy Hackl, Godmother of the Metaverse

What once was a dream of pushing the boundaries of technology and human interaction became a reality for me in 2022. I found myself ringing the opening bell at NASDAQ's market site in the metaverse and the physical world at the same time. I knew in the core of my being that this was just the beginning of an amazing journey. It wasn't just a moment in history; it was also a moment of celebration for women in tech, and one of the people that I wanted by my side was Sandy Carter.

I met Sandy almost a decade ago when she had just launched one of her prior books and I was just getting started in my tech career. Little did I know Sandy would become my mentor, friend, and even boss a couple of years later. Here's an image of Sandy and I opening the markets in the physical and virtual worlds on June 17, 2022.

As one of the first chief metaverse officers in the world, I am often asked what is the definition of the metaverse and when should we venture in it? Although we are still creating, exploring, and understanding it, the metaverse waits for trailblazers like Sandy Carter. It is voices like hers that need to be heard in the tech world. When we worked together at AWS, I learned a lot from her. One thing that will forever remain with me was when she said, "If you can see it, you can be it." This saying has marked my life and is one of the reasons I do what I do now. To say I wouldn't be here if it weren't with Sandy is a fact. So when she asked me to write this foreword, I knew the only answer was ABSOLUTELY!

With the turn of every page, I found myself amazed with the amount of passion and knowledge that Sandy poured out in harnessing the metaverse mindset and sharing it with others. She answers your questions before you can even ask them and leads you to view the web3, the metaverse and AI with a fresh approach and unique perspective.

This book provides the reader a guide on the various ways one can build world-class experiences and strategies within web3, the metaverse and AI. Sandy addresses the potential challenges and gives resources to assist you in developing a plan that best fits your brand or company. With her extensive knowledge of emerging technologies and experience with tactical insight, she helps one to relate to the processes involved with exploring the metaverse through her storytelling.

For those on edge about stepping into the metaverse, allow Sandy to take you on a journey of all the opportunities that are available to you in the metaverse. Don't just be an observer; become a forerunner of this great, new reality. This book is the key to unlocking what comes next for you, just like meeting Sandy unlocked what came next for me many years ago.

Preface

I love emerging technology. Knowing that the best use cases haven't been created yet and that there is no playbook energizes me. My nickname is "the energizer bunny" because these new areas keep me going and going. My career has been spent here. I love helping to shape the future of what will impact our lives.

Having worked on ecommerce, service-oriented architecture (SOA) (note: my first best-selling book was about SOA), social media, cloud, artificial intelligence, smart cities, Internet of Things (IoT), virtual reality (VR), and more, I went down the rabbit hole with Web3 and the metaverse when they first emerged.

It started while I was at Amazon Web Services (AWS), and I saw our customers using AI, blockchain for financial services, supply chain, and even Web3 use cases shown at our reinvent conference. Coinbase, *a secure online platform for buying, selling, transferring, and storing cryptocurrency*, first spoke at reinvent, our AWS conference, in 2018.

In December 2021, I came to a company missioned to deliver digital identity for Web3 and the metaverse and using AI tools. Since I left AWS, it was intriguing to the media. Several stories came out—one from the

New York Times—about the fact that I had left a great company that I loved to focus on these new spaces.

My lightbulb moment came when I received 1000s of emails, direct messages (DMs), Telegrams (TG), What's App, and texts about a single question: "What is Web3 and the metaverse?" and "What does AI matter?"

As a result, I found a lot of my time was spent teaching and keynoting about this space. I've spoken at Davos, CES, SXSW, Web Summit, Abu Dhabi Web3 Government Con, Token 2049, NFT New York, Los Angeles, Miami, ETH Paris, Columbia Business School, and more all answering questions for brands, companies, entities, and governments about why these new technologies are important. I started a group called Unstoppable Women of Web3 and the metaverse to educate more women and diverse groups to ensure we had all voices heard while inventing the next generation of the internet. We won best of show at CES for our group's mission, and two Lovies for our work building a headquarters in the metaverse.

My vision for this book is to share with you, in a fun way, my learnings from speaking to 1000s of companies, universities, countries, believers, and skeptics as well as building in the space—in Web3, the metaverse and AI. My superpower is sharing stories. So, when Wiley asked me to write a business fable about Web3, the metaverse and AI, I eagerly agreed.

I want to hear from you on your learnings as together, this next generation of the internet will be experiential built on all of our insights.

You can reach me at TheRabbitTeam@gmail.com.

Introduction

The internet was created to bring us together. But somewhere along the way, that vision was lost. We handed our data over to centralized figures, allowed big tech to thrive off our creations, and accepted our place in a system that is seemingly out of our control. However, in the far corners of the internet, a new story is being written. The authors are not big tech. No. The authors are you and me. Some of the learnings in this book will center around Web3, AI, and the future of business while creating a metaverse mindset. Let this be your on-ramp to the future of the digital world.

This book is divided into two parts. The first part is a fable. In a fun way, it walks through the concepts of the players in the creation of the new strategy for a fictitious company, EdgyMaven. EdgyMaven could be any company in any industry; its industry is intentionally vague so that the concepts can be applied by business-to-business and business-to-consumer companies of all different industries. This part shows you how EdgyMaven applies concepts, learned by diving in headfirst and playing in the metaverse and using AI tools. It is meant to show that this is a new and emerging space. Although you will see them use the model of the second part, time and again they are reminded that they are creating the playbook as they go as well.

The second part of the book abstracts out the process that Edgy-Maven team went through, showing the five emPOWERments of harnessing the power of Web3, AI, and the metaverse. Worksheets will help you think through building out the team in a way that is far different than how teams are built today. It outlines the concept of a rinse-and-repeat strategy, execution plan, and business case. It does not dictate what to do but is meant to be taken as a guide, as we are in the early days of Web3, AI, and the metaverse. Some of this future playbook will be written by you.

I look forward to hearing your thoughts and how you add to this metaverse mindset and playbook for the future.

PART
I
The Fable

V was the first to suggest new and innovative ways to engage Edgy-Maven's customers. She was totally customer obsessed.

"gm," she exclaimed to the team as they met for the first time. (gm stands for "good morning," but in the Web3, Metaverse, and AI world, it is more than a greeting—it expresses that idea that "we are early" and our future is bright.) "Let's get ready to go down this rabbit hole!"

For hard core Web3, Metaverse, and AI lovers, going down the rabbit hole often involves learning about new and complex business concepts and delving into the technical details of how these technologies work. It can be a fascinating and rewarding experience for those who are interested in the potential of Web3, Metaverse, and AI technologies to disrupt traditional systems and create new opportunities.

That's why V was selected to help figure out how EdgyMaven brand would improve its customer experience, including exploration of the new internet. To be successful, the technical, product, strategy, and marketing teams needed to work together to present solutions to the board. They had asked for some out-of-the-box thinking with new technologies like Web3, Metaverse, and AI to achieve the company's goals.

While she was only recently appointed the chief growth officer, Victoria McSay, known as V to her colleagues, recognized the potential of the new approaches, technology, and the concept of community to help them understand the customer emPOWERment of the new internet.

But they only had a few months to get ready. So, they had to move with a strong bias for action.

"Let's go!" she was heard saying as the meeting began.

1

Getting Started

Backstory

EdgyMaven had been on top of the ratings for customer experience for the five short years it had been in business. In fact, it had won numerous awards for how engaged its community was, how many "love" notes it had received on its team's support and how much its customers were "selling" to other prospects for it. In fact, sometimes it felt like the team didn't have to do any marketing at all!

However, somewhere along the way, leadership got overconfident in the company's success. They started depending on surveys, and the executive team didn't have time for customer meetings. Even though they were located in the heart of innovation—Austin, Texas—they had stopped innovating on the experience that they delivered. Once leading in experiences through new and emerging tech, EdgyMaven was now viewed as being behind the curve.

Customer experience is the last form of true competitive advantage. And with EdgyMaven now struggling in that area, they had brought in V to help them reshape the way that they thought about the customer and how to serve them best leveraging some of the concepts of the new internet.

The New Internet

The new internet was a nebulous concept to be sure. Some called it Web3 or the metaverse with a little bit of artificial intelligence (AI) sprinkled on it. It was always explained in tech terms. Since the user experience of the new internet is much more immersive, V wanted to dive deep to really understand its potential power. Currently, most in the company didn't understand it.

While many of EdgyMaven's competitors had begun experimenting with some of the areas, EdgyMaven had stayed away from it. The concepts of the new internet were interesting to V, and she thought to EdgyMaven as well.

The new internet was based on decentralization as a core concept derived from blockchain. Blockchain is a publicly accessible digital ledger used to store and transfer information without the need for a central authority. Literally, it is a chain of blocks. V made the analogy that it was like a set of storage units, with each storage unit holding information under a key. Since different people own the keys, no one entity or person has access to control all the data stored in the storage units. Decentralization itself refers to replacing systems under a single entity's control with systems that distribute control among participants.

That also meant it was a paradigm shift. It was about the redistribution of power with a goal to improve how societies function. The norm today was a central authority that controls who can use the system. Today, while some have access, many do not.

The shift of the new internet was to be inclusive: excluding no one and allowing billions more to participate in the economy, expand creative opportunity, and build more useful products. Part of the inclusivity meant that individuals owned their own data. And that's where Web3 came in. Web3 is an open movement to broadly decentralize the internet, allowing for individual ownership of identity and personal data. This "digital identity" was owned by each person, including all the data about them. Web3 is seen as potentially bridging the gap between an individual's physical identity and their digital identity. This suggests that everyone will have a "digital identity," which encompasses both their online and real-world legal versions.

And finally, the new internet had a new experience layer called the metaverse. The metaverse had started to become fundamental to everyday existence. It's where we can live, work, interact, and play—from anywhere and at any time—digitally using a lot of new technologies. All of these concepts contained AI tool "help" or partnering.

Eventually the average person will use the metaverse as much as people use the internet and smartphones today. For example, a life-like AI assistant will be your day-to-day companion. Most people will depend on one. It will constantly predict what you want to do next and make suggestions throughout the day. It will give personalized answers to your questions based on your goals, interests, and career paths. Others will immerse themselves in new worlds or learn through doing things in the augmented reality world, instead of just "hearing" about the concepts from a teacher. Studies showed the experiential learning was retained 40% longer.

The metaverse provides many benefits to businesses:

- 3D shared experiences, so workers can collaborate in the same place, no matter where they are based in the physical world with the help of AI.
- New products can be developed in the metaverse, built by remote teams, but still being able to experiment and test in a collaborative 3D space with AI assistance for consolidation of data.
- Collaboration spaces where the languages of team members all over the globe can be translated in real time, eliminating barriers among international teams.

And new jobs will be created from the number of people necessary to build these benefits, as well as the new businesses and use cases that will only be possible in a fully realized virtual world.

The metaverse brought in not only new experience technologies but new ways to meet your future customer.

AI was embedded throughout. It was a tool that teams would use to create content, analyze customer data and behavior to personalize marketing campaigns, make product recommendations, and predict future customer needs. As V liked to call it—augmented intelligence due to the AI tools augmenting her team's work.

This mattered to EdgyMaven's core principle of inclusivity and great experiences.

Why V Matters

Leadership always matters. V was hired for her learning and be curious superpower. She had a dear friend who used to work at Amazon that explained it so well from the Amazon Leadership Principles. Leaders are never done learning and always seek to improve themselves. They are curious about new possibilities and act to explore them. The world today is constantly changing and moving quickly, and if you don't learn new things, you are already left behind.

V loved the book by Lewis Carroll called *Through the Looking-Glass*. She read it to her daughter and had fallen in love with a particular quote: "My dear, here we must run as fast as we can, just to stay in place. And if you wish to go anywhere you must run twice as fast as that." This is known as the Red Queen theory to business, and V fancied herself as that Red Queen now.

V was the perfect person for this role. She had already researched hundreds of companies in the space and had learned three important things.

First, this new technology was real. For example, blockchain had been around for 10 years. Blockchain has grown to be a bedrock of the worldwide record-keeping systems, including Web2 systems like supply chain and financial services, and now was the backbone of Web3 and the metaverse.

Second, these new technologies was already disrupting companies and markets. Fashion was a hot area for the metaverse, and already young designers felt like it was cooler to be a designer for virtual designs, not those in the real world.

Disrupt or Be Disrupted

The first thing to remember about disruption is either you are the disrupter or you are being disrupted. This is true for every company in every industry. Companies that are intimidated by new technology, or simply ignorant on how to use it, get easily disrupted. If you're the leader and you don't have time to explore something new, ensure that someone in your company is at least looking into it. It's better to know a little bit about a new technology than nothing and get blindsided.

Consumer behavior, like technology, is constantly evolving, like technology. People are consuming more content on their mobile devices than they are on their TVs, computers, and radio combined. The activities you're doing now in your business should be different than they were last year because things change that fast. What worked a year ago isn't going to work the same today, tomorrow, or next year. Evolve or die.

Third, this Web3, AI, and metaverse space is creating a gazillion opportunities. V's daughter suggested that V stop using the word "lots" and started using "gazillion" because she said that she'd heard her mom talk about it so much. V had always followed the developers because where they build innovation, magic happens. According to the "Electric Capital Developer Report," she found that the highest number of developers in history according to the document had begun developing for Web3, the Metaverse and AI. Moreover, the report pointed out that 65% of active developers and 45% of full-time developers started working on Web3 with more now diving into AI.

However, this wasn't V's first rodeo either. She knew that it was the early days of this technology. She's heard it said that "Web3 was in the dial-up" phase, meaning just like the start of the internet didn't have high-speed connection but old and slow dial-up connection, we were in the first phase of the space. That typically meant that an education component was needed as well as more focus on user interface (UI) and design capability to make it easy.

She would go into this adventure with her eyes wide open. Her plan was to make magic from the innovation that the next internet was bringing through Web3, AI, and the metaverse for EdgyMaven's customers. She was, after all, customer obsessed.

It's Not Just About the Tech

"Wow," said V over lunch to her colleagues. "I'm reading this new Gartner report, and it says that it won't be long before a quarter of the world spends more than an hour each day in the metaverse, with the metaverse being in the list of the top 10 new technologies that all companies should explore." She paused to take a sip of tea and then continued. "And Bloomberg Intelligence analysts forecast the scope for market opportunity is around the $800 billion mark. AI will be even larger. So, to really dive deep on this game-changing topic, I need to step back and look at the bigger approach and then build the right team."

First, she needed to help her team ascend a complex learning curve. Education was going to be critical to her success. And not just technology education. She needed to provide them education on the use cases and business value brought to the table. She didn't want the team to rush into the space with hopes of this edgy new tech quickly changing their customer experience. Without a solid understanding of the space, they may mis-invest and have little to show for it.

Second, she wanted to set a bold vision for the space based on their use cases, or the why. This step means to deeply understand what a game changer would be. EdgyMaven needed to state the business goals of a presence in Web3, Metaverse and AI. For example, would it be the ability to interact with their community in a new and innovative way? Or would it be tying their real-world asset to maximize their awareness to a new audience and increase value over time?

VALUE FIRST

A great example of focusing first on value to a community is Tiffany and Company. They partnered with CryptoPunks, a hip and cool NFT collection. An NFT is a non-fungible token or digital asset. These digital assets lived on the blockchain. Tiffany and company linked the sale of 250 necklace pendants to those who were owners of the digital asset, the CryptoPunks. Tiffany management did their research into what and how to bridge their value in luxury jewelry to an NFT. The result of creating value was a quick and profitable sellout.

Third, V had to create and grow the right team for this strategy. With Web3, AI, and the metaverse being built by so many in real time, it was challenging to see where it was heading. In her mind, she determined that she needed the following architypes: the educator, the gamer, the product manager, the strategist, marketer, and technologist.

- **The Educator.** While education was important internally, it would also be important externally. She wanted someone who was passionate about evangelizing to the audience in a way that they would understand.
- **The Gamer.** Experimentation is key. To participate in Web3, you must be in Web3, Metaverse and AI. She wanted someone who lived it already. For example, V needed someone who would jump in and create an avatar, build the digital identity, and buy property in the metaverse while leverage AI.
- **The Product Manager.** Product management is about connecting the idea to the offering. Balancing constraints between creativity and strategy alignment is a critical step to authentic meaningful Web3, Metaverse and AI experiences.
- **The Strategist.** While V was great at developing strategic plans, she wanted an out-of-the-box thinker to assist her in crafting the company strategy.
- **The Marketer.** V was going to look for a marketer who raised the bar on creativity and didn't have to have a playbook written. She wanted someone who wanted to create the playbook. She knew that highly developed marketing departments have a great pulse on their audience, which can be leveraged for this research effort.
- **The Technologist.** Technology would not be the first step, but it would be a crucial step. Everything had to be thought through from user interface to interoperability. She wanted someone who already knew blockchain, Web3, and AI. Her

preference was someone who also knew gaming, AI or the metaverse from the technical side too.

And she needed a governance model that would rally the company on this big bold vision. In her mind, a governance model is a framework for establishing accountability, roles, and decision-making authority. It included the established team who would weigh in on all decisions.

Finally, a very important part of her framework was exploration and experimentation. She wanted the team going "down the rabbit hole" and testing things out. And this would lead them back to building their learning and be curious muscle that would enable them to reiterate on their vision and execution. In fact, she would build a rabbit team first. The team was called the rabbit team as they were headed down the rabbit hole. (In Web3 speak, the rabbit hole is where you dive deep into a subject. It is taken from *Alice in Wonderland* because it describes the experience people have when they begin to look inside the complicated, confusing world of Web3.)

She really liked that name. The first rabbit team!

With these elements in place on her pad, she would go back to the chief executive officer (CEO) Monday to walk her through the approach. But she had one more item to cover. The CEO would ask about the biggest challenges that she would face.

The Challenges

Taking a day to get outside and walk her dogs, have coffee with friends, and spend time with her family, V never failed to bring a notepad with her. She would often comment that "Memory is fallible. When you have a good idea, write it down immediately. My best ideas come in the shower, walking, or in the gym. I always keep a notepad ready."

While V would face many challenges, her top four that she had to address were the following, with the first one really being the biggest.

- It was early. V wanted to make sure that they were experimenting along their journey and that the company understood it was early. She knew that there would be failures along the way and wanted to ensure that the rabbit team and her company recognized that fact as well. Several things were blocking the widespread adoption of Web3, Metaverse and AI. Since Web3, Metaverse and AI are complex, it was often difficult for the average person to understand. This could make it difficult for people to get involved and use these technologies. Her team would have to conquer that challenge. In addition, she knew that there was a lack of interoperability among the metaverse ecosystems, making it difficult to easily switch between metaverses. She was hopeful that the Open Metaverse Alliance (OMA3) would address some of these items but knew it would take time.

  OMA3 is a consortium of the leading Web3 and metaverse firms that have come together to solve the industry's interoperability issues. In a nutshell, OMA3 aims to create uniform standards and ease access across all Web3 and metaverse platforms.

- Navigating emerging innovations in a new customer experience strategy would pose a challenge for managing, communicating, and equipping the internal team. V felt very confident here with her three-week plan, including her "PlayStorm" where the team would immerse themselves into the whole space. (Some would call this a Brainstorm but V wanted them to PlayStorm instead!)

- Achieving fluency in this emerging space would require sharp skills and the ability to craft relatable analogies for customers, like an acrobat. Just as her team would be challenged in learning the emerging concepts, V had to find a way to ensure her customers understood them as well. While there were about 26% of consumers who had played with a Web3 wallet, metaverse, AI, or NFT, EdgyMaven had to understand its customers' fluency and meet them where they were. The meant that education was an unusual critical success factor.

- Defining business outcomes in a brand new technology space is like a game of darts in the dark—it requires precision, adaptability, and a willingness to learn from missed marks. Since this was an emerging space, with lots of experimentation required, V's challenge was how would be in the metrics she used to rate their success. This was on her mind as she wanted to truly identify the areas that had improved for her customers with the plan they executed.

She wrote everything down on a piece of paper, ready for her discussion. But she wanted to sleep on it one more night to tweak any new ideas that came to mind in the morning.

We're Ready

In the morning, V finalized her approach for Web3, AI, and the metaverse and was ready for her presentation at the CEO meeting. This was just an initial meeting to walk through the rabbit team selection, the research and analysis she would do, and the plan for education before developing the strategy. The proposed strategy, of course, would align with the company's overall vision and goals and would be designed to ensure that the company stayed ahead of the curve in terms of technology adoption and innovation. And of course, she would have to address the challenges that she could.

While the final review would consist of a projected timeline and budget, this discussion would be about the way she would decide on that plan. With all the necessary preparations in place and her challenges on paper, V prepared to meet her CEO to explain the way forward.

2 | The Team

The Meeting

With her framework in hand, and her challenges on paper, V prepared to meet her CEO to explain the way forward.

V, the chief growth officer at EdgyMaven, sat down with CEO Steph Williams to discuss the selection of the team she had assembled to explore the technology and business model changes in Web3, the Metaverse and AI space. In addition, V wanted to share her overall approach.

"I'm really happy with the team I put together," V said. "We have a great mix of skills and expertise, including a skilled gamer, an educator, a product manager, a strategist, a marketer, and a designer."

Steph nodded in agreement. "That's great to hear. I know we're all excited about the potential of Web3, AI, and the metaverse, but it's important that we have the right team in place to explore these changes. I want to make it clear that this is not a technology project. This is a project to use the technology to solve real-world problems we are having around customer experience and engagement."

"Absolutely," V replied. "One of the things I focused on when building the team was finding people with diverse perspectives. We have team members with backgrounds in engineering, marketing, and design, which will prove to be a valuable asset in our problem-solving process."

"I also made sure to choose team members who are a good fit for our company culture and have strong communication skills," V continued. "It's important that the team can work well together and effectively communicate their progress to the rest of the organization."

Steph nodded in agreement. "I couldn't agree more. And I know the team is excited about the potential of these technologies and are eager to explore its business applications."

"Exactly," V said with a smile. "I think we have the right team in place to push back on defining the Web3, Metaverse, and AI strategy for our company, and I'm confident that we'll be able to come up with some innovative solutions. The overall approach is here, with us spending time getting geared up on knowledge and then actually playing with it, before we start in earnest on building our strategy and execution plan. We are ready to have EdgyMaven put back on top of customer experience and be viewed as an innovator again."

Steph smiled back at V. "I have no doubt that you and your team will get us back on top. I'm looking forward to seeing the results of your work."

Reflection

After her meeting with the CEO, V reflected on her team selection. She had borrowed a framework to select the right skill sets. Since this space was so new, and there really wasn't a 10-year thought-through approach, she was borrowing ideas from those who had at least started before her. She also knew she'd have to create some playbooks from scratch because they just didn't exist.

The first task she had accomplished was ensuring she had the right team, the team she had just shared with her boss.

V used a framework that guided her to select an educator and a gamer, or player, as they were called this space. In addition, she knew she needed product management, strategy, and marketing but from unique perspectives not tied to Web2 approaches, yet knowledgeable about them.

And she needed a technologist/builder or, as they were called in Web3, a buidler This was a technologist who could speak geek and business.

V herself would serve as the change agent, as this was her superpower.

She looked at the sheet of paper where she had assembled a dossier of the team and their unique skills sets.

The Change Agent: V Cary

V is a tech-savvy leader with a passion for turning companies around. With her strong leadership skills and innovative approach to problem-solving, she is not afraid to take on a challenge. She is always looking for ways to leverage technology to streamline processes and drive growth.

Despite the demands of her high-pressure job, V is known for her calm and level-headed demeanor and her ability to inspire and motivate her team.

Whether she's negotiating with investors or strategizing a new product launch, V approaches every task with determination and a clear vision for success.

The Educator: Dawn Alek

V selected Dawn Alek as her educator. Dawn is a young woman with a strong background in education and a deep commitment to helping everyone reach their full potential. She has a master's degree in education from the University of Washington and has been working in the field for over a decade, during which time she has gained a wealth of experience.

As a learning specialist, Dawn is skilled in identifying people's unique learning needs and developing personalized learning plans to help them succeed. She is patient and understanding and is always willing to go the extra mile.

In her free time, Dawn enjoys reading and staying up-to-date on the latest educational research and trends.

The Gamer: Tommy Seaport

Tommy Seaport is a skilled gamer, originally from Cape Town, South Africa.

He has been playing video games for as long as he can remember and has a particular passion for action and adventure games. Tommy is known among his friends and online gaming communities for his quick reflexes and strategic thinking, and he spends many hours each day honing his skills and competing in online tournaments.

In addition to his love of gaming, Tommy is also a huge fan of technology and is always on the lookout for the latest and greatest gadgets and devices. When he's not busy playing games, he can often be found tinkering with computers and experimenting with new software and apps. He had recently started dabbling in the metaverse and became familiar with Roblox, a massive multiplayer online game platform that allows users to create their own games and play games created by other users. It's designed to be accessible to players of all ages.

Despite his love of all things digital, Tommy also enjoys spending time outdoors, and can often be found surfing or hiking like he does in the beautiful South African landscape.

The Product Manager 3.0: Johnny Poyhonan

Johnny Poyhonan is a driven and ambitious product manager from the streets of New York City. With a background in business and marketing, Johnny is skilled at developing and bringing new products to market.

He is a natural leader and excels at managing cross-functional teams, setting clear goals, and ensuring that projects are delivered on time and on budget.

Growing up in the hustle and bustle of the city that never sleeps instilled in Johnny a strong work ethic and a desire to succeed. He is not afraid to roll up his sleeves and put in the hard work necessary to get the job done and is known among his colleagues for his tenacity and dedication.

In his free time, Johnny enjoys exploring the diverse neighborhoods and culture of NYC, trying new restaurants, and staying active with sports and fitness.

The Strategist: Melissa Pop

Melissa Pop is a strategic thinker with a strong background in technology. She spent several years working for Amazon Web Services (AWS), where she gained valuable experience in AI and cloud computing and helped clients around the world leverage the power of the AWS platform. As a strategist, Melissa excels at analyzing complex problems and developing creative solutions. She is known for her ability to think outside the box and bring a fresh perspective to challenges faced by her clients. In her current role, Melissa is using her skills and expertise to help businesses and organizations make data-driven decisions and achieve their goals.

In addition to her professional accomplishments, Melissa is also a proud mother of two young sons. She is dedicated to being a hands-on mother and making sure that her children have the support and guidance they need to succeed in life.

Despite the demands of parenting and her career, Melissa also makes time for herself and enjoys staying active through yoga and running.

The Marketer: Emma Sphynx

Emma Sphynx is a marketing leader with a strong background. She graduated from Duke University with a degree in marketing and has since built a successful career in the field working for companies like Reddit, Microsoft, and Nike.

Emma is known for her confidence, creativity, and ability to think outside the box. As a natural leader and motivator, she inspires her team to achieve their best work and is always looking for new ways to innovate.

In her free time, Emma enjoys spending time outdoors, particularly on hikes through beautiful natural surroundings. With her combination of brains and brawn, Emma is a force to be reckoned with in the marketing world.

The Technologist: Greg Dashed

Greg is a technology pioneer known for his bold and sassy approach to innovation. He has a reputation for leading the way into new and untested areas of technology, such as blockchain and AI. His friends call him "Dash."

Greg is not afraid to challenge the status quo and is always looking for ways to push the boundaries of what is possible. He is knowledgeable in blockchain and Web3. And of course, he has dabbled with AI and the metaverse. Many thought he could be the next Steve Wozniak!

With his sharp mind and unapologetic attitude, he has made a name for himself as a leader in the tech industry. Whether he's developing a new product or giving a presentation to a room full of executives, Greg approaches every challenge with confidence and a sense of fun.

In his free time, he builds robots and competes in several well-known robot competitions.

The First Get-together

As the team gathered in the conference room, V began the meeting.

"Good morning, everyone. Thank you for joining me today. We have a big task ahead of us, and I'm excited to have each and every one of you on board to help us achieve our goal."

Dawn Alek, the educator, interjected, "V, before we get started, can you give us more information about what we're trying to accomplish here? I want to make sure we're all on the same page."

V nodded, "Of course, Dawn. We are looking to build Web3, the Metaverse, and AI strategy for our company, hopefully taking advantage of AI tools as we go. We need to stay ahead of the curve in the tech industry, and this is the next step for us. We'll be working closely with Tommy Seaport, our gamer, to understand the gaming aspect of the metaverse, and with Johnny Poyhonan, our product manager 3.0, to develop and launch our products include AI Tools. Melissa Pop, our strategist, will be working on analyzing the market and developing a plan, and Emma Sphynx, our marketer, will be responsible for promoting and branding our products. And we cannot forget our technologist, Greg Dashed."

Tommy Seaport, who was known for his quick reflexes and strategic thinking, spoke up, "I'm excited to be a part of this team. I've been following the development of the metaverse for a while now, and I can't wait to see how we can leverage it for our company."

Johnny Poyhonan, the product manager 3.0, added, "I agree with Tommy. The metaverse has huge potential, and I can't wait to see how we can use it to drive growth for our company. And I cannot wait to continue to grow my skills with the newest AI tools out there."

Melissa Pop, the strategist, chimed in, "I've been researching the market, and I think there's a lot of opportunity here. We just need to make sure we're making data-driven decisions and staying ahead of the curve."

"I agree," said Emma Sphynx, the marketer. "We need to be innovative and think outside the box when it comes to promoting and branding our products in the metaverse."

V nodded. "Excellent, it sounds like we all understand the task at hand. Here's how I propose we get started. I'd like to have us all brought up to speed on the technology and the use cases in this space. I have the perfect person to get us started. And then I'd like us to leverage a framework that has worked for several companies in defining their change in branding, community, and engagement and experiences leveraging those new technologies. Let's see if there is a fit for EdgyMaven in accomplishing our overall goals."

As the team began to discuss and strategize, Greg Dashed, the technologist, who was known for his bold and sassy approach to innovation, added, "I'm excited to be a part of this team and can't wait to see how we can push the boundaries of what is possible with the metaverse technology."

V smiled. "I couldn't have said it better myself, Greg. Let's get to work and make this happen. But first let's start with a little brainstorming so that we will be ready for the next step."

Team Brainstorming

"I practically invented brainstorming," bragged Tommy. "I'll lead. Our overall goal is to find out how to drive better customer engagement and loyalty. The theory is that we could achieve this best by defining a metaverse and Web3 strategy for our company using AI tools. We have been tasked with creating a comprehensive plan that will help us stay ahead of the curve and take advantage of the opportunities that this new technology presents."

Dawn paused the brainstorm. "Before we start, can someone explain to me what the metaverse is and how it relates to Web3?"

"Sure," piped in Johnny. "I know that we have more to learn but at a high level, the metaverse is a virtual world where people can interact and engage with each other, and it's powered by Web3 technology. It's the next step in the evolution of the internet, and it's going to change the way we interact with each other and with technology."

"And Web3 is the technology that enables the metaverse," continued Melissa, who had clearly being doing her homework too. "It's a decentralized network that allows for the creation of decentralized applications, or dApps. It's a new way of building and using technology that's more secure and more efficient than traditional methods."

"So, what does that have to do with customer experience?" interrupted Emma. "This is not a tech problem. This is a solution problem. It's going to take a 360-degree approach to do this right."

"That's a great question, Emma," said Greg. "We can use the metaverse to create new and unique experiences for our customers. For example, companies have created virtual shopping malls where customers can shop and interact with our products in a more immersive way. There are also ways that companies have used digital twin or industrial metaverse for training their customers to understand the value of their products using AI. We could also use the metaverse to create new forms of entertainment, such as virtual reality games or experiences for our products.

"But wait, before going too far, I think we need to tag a space for big idea around our current offerings. Can't we use Web3, AI, and the metaverse to enhance our existing products and services too? For example, we could use Web3 technology to create a more secure and efficient way of conducting transactions on our e-commerce platform."

"Okay, as long as we are framing our strategy needs," Emma broke in, "we should also think about how we can use the metaverse and AI to improve the way we educate and train our employees and customers. Imagine being able to create virtual classrooms or training sessions that are more engaging and interactive."

"I agree," pitched in Melissa. "We should also think about how we can use the metaverse and AI to gather data and insights on our customers and their behavior. This could help us make better decisions and improve our products and services."

"So, it sounds like we have a lot of ideas and opportunities to explore," said Johnny. "We should focus on identifying the most promising opportunities and developing a plan to take advantage of them."

Emma continued the thought, "And we should also think about how we can market and promote our products and services in the metaverse. We need to make sure that we're reaching the right audience and communicating the value of our offerings in an effective way. We should also think about how we can use the metaverse to build our brand and reputation. It's a new and exciting space, and we could establish ourselves as leaders in the industry."

V had been listening intently. If this was the passion and energy this team had, they would have a great time nailing the education and then the plan. But they were already coming up with solutions. They need to understand the space first, and she meant, really understand it.

Tommy interrupted her thoughts, "All right, so it sounds like we have a lot of work to do. Let's use this framework to start by identifying the most promising opportunities and developing a plan to take advantage of them. We'll need to work together as a team and use our diverse skills and expertise to make this happen."

"And let's not forget," commented Emma, "that the AI and metaverse and Web3 technology is still in its early stages, so we need to be prepared to adapt and evolve as the technology and market develops."

V paused the team. "This is what a great team looks like! Collaborating and already defining the opportunities. But let's not get ahead of ourselves around the solutions. There will be time for that. Let me explain how I'd like to approach this challenge."

The Next Step

The team would spend the next several weeks working closely together, learning about Web3, AI, and the metaverse. Then they would spend a week immersing themselves in it. And only then would they start to develop a strategy to leverage it for the company and review it with the board.

Even with their diverse skills and expertise, the task ahead seemed big. They would be challenged with coming up with innovative solutions, with the help of AI tools, and eventually launching a successful Web3 and metaverse approach to have stronger customer experience and engagement.

If they did this right, the company's growth could soar, and they would be able to stay ahead of the curve in the tech industry

But it would be hard. A friend of V's, Fred Swaniker, the head of the African Leadership Group (ALG) always said, "Do hard things." The ALG is a globally recognized pre-university program that identifies high potential youth across the African continent and then develops their leadership and entrepreneurial skills in a two-year diploma program that empowers each of them for a lifetime of impact. Fred himself had been named by *Forbes* as one of the 10 youngest power men in Africa.

V's team was also up for the toughest challenge.

As she sent the team home, she decided to share a quote to motivate them. V loved quotes. She found them inspirational because they often encapsulate a powerful message or idea in a simple and memorable way. For her, quotes helped her to see things from a different perspective. They served as a reminder of important values and helped to keep her focused on her goals and aspirations.

The quote she shared was from Sandy Carter, modified from a famous quote by Margaret Mead about citizens: "Never doubt that a small group of innovative, committed people can change the world; indeed, it's the only thing that ever has."

"You guys are that group of innovative and committed people who can change the world!!! Let's make history—and have some fun while we do it! I'll see you back here tomorrow at 9 a.m. for a bright and early start." With that, she closed the session for the day.

Deep Tissue

With the selection of this diverse team, V thought about the deep tissue that this team brought to the table and about her ability to bring together a group of individuals with a wide range of skills and expertise. Deep tissue to V meant a comprehensive and thorough approach to addressing strategy for the digital ecosystem of Web3, Metaverse and AI. It would involve understanding and addressing the underlying technical and social structures that make up the Web3, Metaverse and AI landscape. This rabbit team would need to develop a strategy that could draw upon the strengths and address the challenges of this new digital paradigm.

Tommy, the skilled gamer, brought his quick reflexes and strategic thinking to the table, while Dawn, the educator, brought a deep understanding of learning and development.

Johnny, the product manager, brought his ability to develop and bring new products to market, and Melissa, the strategist, brought her expertise in technology and data analysis.

Emma, the marketer, brought her experience in marketing and creativity, while Greg, the designer, brought his design skills and ability to think outside the box.

V thought to herself, "Together, this team can tackle any challenge that comes their way, using their diverse perspectives and skills to find innovative solutions. If they worked well together, they would have a positive impact on the company culture."

It seemed like it would be a great team structure, and she was thankful for the framework that guided her on the right skills, along with passion for the technology they would be exploring.

V thought to herself, "This combination of skills, expertise, and personalities is what makes this team so important. The success in their exploration of the technology and its potential business applications is that we have the perfect rabbit team set!"

3 | Learn and Be Curious— The Tech

The Education Begins

V brought in an evangelist from EdSuccess, a company devoted to educating corporate brands on new and emerging technology, to help train her team about all the new technology. Rex Williams was an expert in emerging technology and linking them to business outcomes.

He was selected because he was a storyteller/teacher. A storyteller is a great teacher because storytelling is a powerful and engaging way to communicate ideas and concepts. They use vivid language, descriptive details, and expressive gestures to bring the story to life, which can make the material more interesting and memorable for the listener.

In addition, stories make concepts that are hard to grasp more relatable and easier to understand than a word-driven explanation. For example, a story shows how a particular concept or idea works in a real-world situation, making it easier to grasp the concept. Overall, storytelling is an effective teaching tool because it helps capture the attention and imagination of the listener, making the learning process more enjoyable and effective.

True to his reputation, Rex began the weeklong session with a story. "I arrived in Austin yesterday," he said. "As I was walking down the street, I saw this bottle on the road. I reached down and picked it up. And then I rubbed the bottle and out popped a genie. Now this really happened," he said, as a few people chuckled. "This genie said to me, 'Rex, this is your lucky day! Not only do you get to be at EdgyMaven, but you get three wishes. However, there is a catch.'" Rex snickered. "You know there's always a catch! The genie continued, 'Whatever you wish for, your evil archenemy gets double.' So, I thought about it for a minute and said. 'Okay. Here are my three wishes.'"

Rex paused for effect.

"First, I wish for a red Tesla X because who doesn't want a red Tesla. But—poof!—my evil archenemy got two. For my second wish, I thought about how much I loved Austin, so I wished for a house on Lake Austin but—poof!—my evil archenemy got two houses. So, for my final wish, I said, 'Genie, please scare me half to death.'"

After pausing for the laughter, Rex continued. "Why do I tell you that story? Well, it's not to scare you half to death, but I do have three wishes for this session today. First, I'd like to familiarize you all with the technology of the new internet. Second, I'd like to share use cases to show you the business outcomes companies have seen from usage already. Finally, I'd like to help you figure out some of the challenges you will face." He concluded his opening story, looking into the eyes of the rabbit team ready to get started. Everyone nodded with approval, urging him to continue.

The Word Picture

Rex started by giving a bit of background on how he learned about the space. "In the last year, I've spoken to about 400 different companies, investors, accelerators, and skeptics about the new internet. I'll share that insight today but these are three big things that I took away from those conversations.

"First, regardless of what you call it, this space is real. There are enterprises using the technology today and in big numbers. Second, the new internet is already disrupting businesses today, and in the future, it will disrupt even more markets and businesses. We are already seeing that in fashion, learning, and gaming with many more industries to come. Third, more and more brands are entering the space to experiment. Those early adopters will be miles ahead of those who wait. However, there are areas to improve upon, too, because we are in the dial-up phase of Web3, the metaverse and AI."

As he paused, Melissa raised her hand, "What do you mean by the dial-up phase?" As the strategist of the team, Melissa always was looking for the significance to their strategic approach. She had learned during her time at AWS that understanding anything customer related was part of the customer obsession journey.

"Well," he explained. "The dial-up was the first phase of the internet we currently have today. In the dial-up days of the internet, people used a phone line to connect their computers to the internet," he exclaimed, as many in the room gasped out loud. "To connect to the internet, you would need a modem, which is a device that connects your computer to a phone line. When you wanted to go online, you would dial a phone number that connected you to your internet provider. What that did was make so you couldn't use the phone when you were online and the speed was very slow. Because it was so slow, it took a long time to do simple tasks like downloading files or streaming videos."

"But despite these limitations, dial-up was an important part in the development of the internet as we know it today. It was one of the first ways that people could connect to the internet from their homes, and it paved the way for the faster, more reliable broadband connections that are common today."

"So, what's our modem problem today?" asked Tommy, eager to know what he was up against. His gaming skills and familiarity with the space made his questions often deep in the challenges they were up against.

"Well, there are a few, so I'll just go through the big ones," Rex said. "First, there is a big gap in user interface. As we go through it, you will see that it can be a bit hard. We need to ensure education is at the top of the chart as the developers work through making it easier."

"Second, there are still some areas that are expensive. For example, if we placed all the data on the blockchain, it would cost us too much. Therefore, many call what we are doing Web 2.5, not Web3 yet, as much of the Web2 technology still need enduring.

"And third is scale. Given that it's new, there is room for improvement in scaling as well. Scaling technology refers to changing the size or capacity of something. For example, software developers use scaling technology to make a website or app work faster or handle more traffic. Scaling helps us make things that are the right size, speed, or capacity for different purposes." Rex finally took a deep breath to pause. "Any questions before we go to the next section?"

No one asked a question. V wondered if it was because they were overwhelmed with the data or if they were just too shy to ask questions yet.

So, Rex continued, "Next, we are going to go deeper down the rabbit hole. That's Web3 speak for diving deep into the space itself!"

And the ice was broken. They all laughed as those were the first words that they had heard from their fearless leader too! V was finally becoming more trusted by the team!

Down the Rabbit Hole

Rex showed the following picture and began to break it down. This picture was created by Ray Wang, CEO and founder of Constellation, with collaboration from Sandy Carter.

The Two-sided Marketplace

As the slide was displayed, Rex started his explanation about why this picture was critical to understanding the space.

"The first thing to note on this graphic is that you'll see this two-sided marketplace—one for creators and one for digital networks." Rex pointed to the screen first to the left side and then the right side of the slide.

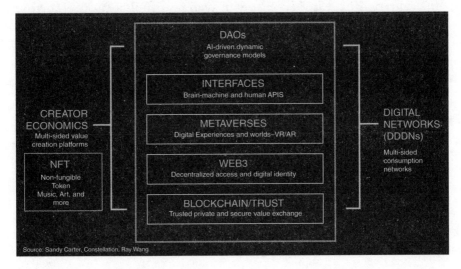

Figure 3.1   The Layer Cake

"On the left side is the Creator Economy. The new internet is the home of the creator. Creators are musicians and artists even entrepreneurs who are builders, designers, and producers creating new ideas. This is one of the differences between the new internet and the old internet. The new internet is opening its arms to these new nontechnical communities."

"A growing number of people are making a living by creating and sharing content on the new internet. This content can take many forms, such as NFTs, avatars, and even music. These creators can earn money through a variety of means, such as advertising revenue, sponsorships, and purchases of 'AI Art' from fans. The rise of the creator economy has been made possible by advances in technology that have made it easier for people to create and share their work online, as well as the growing popularity of metaverse that support these creators.

"In the world of Web2, the creator economy is dominated by a few large platforms, such as YouTube and Facebook, which provide the infrastructure for individuals to share their content, and which often take a significant cut of the revenue generated from that content.

"In contrast, the creator economy in Web3 is centered around the use of decentralized technologies such as blockchain and smart contracts to enable individuals to create and share content without relying on a central platform. We will get to those technologies here in a few seconds," Rex added as he saw puzzlement on some faces, people wondering what those terms meant.

"This allows creators to have more control over their content and the revenue generated from it as well as greater flexibility in how they choose to monetize their content.

"In Web2, a few large companies hold a significant amount of power and control over the content and revenue generated by creators, whereas in Web3, this power is distributed more evenly among creators, their audience, and the technology itself. This decentralization can provide benefits such as greater transparency, improved security, and more equitable distribution of revenue, but it also introduces new challenges such as the need for new infrastructure and business models."

Rex was on a roll and really wanted to get through this section before taking questions.

"Overall, the creator economy represents a shift toward more community-driven models of content creation and monetization, with the potential to offer greater opportunities and autonomy for creators and their audiences." Rex concluded with the left side of the graphic and moved to the right side.

"On the right side are the Digital Networks that serve as multi-sided consumption networks. They create value primarily by enabling direct interactions between two or more customer or participant groups by connecting them together and by helping with interactions and exchanges between these different groups. For example, a metaverse app like Upland connects communities of players, while a marketplace like OpenSea connects buyers and sellers. In both cases, value is created by bringing these groups together and facilitating transactions between them."

Greg, V's technologist, jumped in. "So, the success of a multi-sided consumption network depends on the network effects—where the value increases as more people use it, right? It's kind of the Amazon model of the flywheel," he said, drawing a circle in the air. "The virtuous cycle that drives more users that attracts more producers, which in turn attracts more users."

"That's right, Greg! So there are many business lessons in this flywheel," replied Rex.

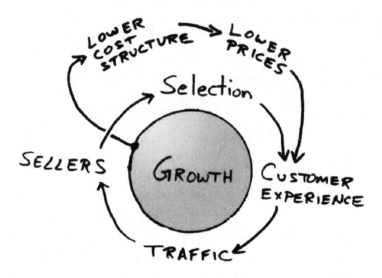

Figure 3.2   Flywheel

In the Middle

After Rex discussed the two-sided marketplace, he moved on to show how the technology "stack" in the middle was driving some of the new business discussions.

"In the middle is the layer cake," Rex said. "Now this is not a strict technical view but more of a marketecture view. This view shows how the pieces fit together to form a powerful stack of technology. We will be beginning at the bottom of that stack."

The Blockchain

"I love the blockchain," gushed Rex. "I think V and I both see a lot of value of this technology. At the lowest level of the view is the blockchain. The blockchain is the backbone of the new internet and is an algorithm that maintains a permanent and tamperproof record of transactional data. It decentralizes how data are maintained and controlled and transforms existing power structures."

"THE BLOCKCHAIN IS THE BACKBONE OF EVERYTHING WEB3 AND THE METAVERSE."

—Sandy Carter

"Did you know that by 2030, blockchain will be the base layer of 90% of the internet," crowed Rex, showing how much of a fan he really was!

"Blockchain is the backbone to all Web3 and the metaverse. The way you can think about blockchains is literally as a chain of blocks. These blocks all are in order and they each have a unique identifier and they're all strung together into this chain.

"What is inside these blocks? The way you can think about these blocks is as storage units so they can store data and in some cases transactions.

"These storage units are run by this decentralized network where each computer represents a storage unit. Each storage unit is locked and can only be accessed with a unique key. When a person wants to store an item in a storage unit, they must first obtain a key to unlock the unit and place the item inside.

"Since that storage unit facility keeps a record of all the transactions that take place within it, including which unit was accessed, when it was accessed, and who accessed it, they secure that knowledge with unique keys required to access the units. Anyone ever watch *Storage Wars*? Yea, me too. *Storage Wars* is a reality television show that aired on the A&E Network from 2010 to 2019. It followed a group of professional buyers who visited storage facilities in California to bid on the contents of abandoned storage units in the hope of finding valuable items to resell. Many times, that had to wait to get into a unit until someone came with a key.

"Just like that storage unit facility keeps a record of all the transactions that take place within it, a blockchain is used to record transactions that take place within a decentralized network. Just as the storage unit facility is secured by the unique keys that are required to access the units, a blockchain is secured by algorithms that ensure the security of the transactions recorded on it."

Rex now paused, knowing that he had just covered a lot of technical thoughts for a pretty much nontechnical audience.

Dawn, the teams' expert educator, jumped in. "So, in essence, no centralized party is providing the role of gatekeeper. Right? And this is very different from the internet today, where each application holds the rights to its data. Did I understand that correctly?" Dawn was constantly studying the trends in education. She was one of the top experts in the field today.

"You nailed it, Dawn," Rex cheered as he high-fived Dawn.

"Today, each application—like Instagram, TikTok, Twitter—has its own private data server that it doesn't share. So, all the data contained within an application is private to that application. In Web3, this model is flipped on its head, and suddenly, all the applications we know and love and use will be built using the same infrastructure using the same backend. This opens the door for tons and tons of new applications being able to log in with one digital identity that you own—not the application—because we're all sharing this same database instead of being siloed into different servers! We're all using the same decentralized network and now your application can be on the same exact playing field as every single other application that's built in Web3." Rex was so excited that he almost missed a question.

Melissa, the expert strategist, raised her hand. "Could you give us an example? I'm a little lost in the technology!" Many in the room nodded, thanking Melissa quietly in their heads for her question.

"Sure!" Rex continued with an example: "Let's think about a normal transaction when I want a cup of coffee. When I buy a cup of coffee and swipe my debit card, the bank—which is a centralized entity—is reducing my account balance when I buy that cup of coffee."

"Ah, I see," said Melissa. "So the question is, 'Where does that transaction get stored?' Right?"

"Exactly," said Rex. "Well, the bank maintains its own private data servers. This information is being stored and validated by the bank. The bank is the holder of the truth. It is the one that maintains the state of our account balances."

"Well how is that different on the blockchain?" asked Tommy, the gamer of the crew, really getting into the groove now.

"Well, a transaction on the blockchain is a bit different," Rex answered. "If I want to go buy a cup of coffee with Bitcoin, which is built on the blockchain, the decentralized network of miners works on the transaction. So now instead of one bank maintaining the state of my account and holding the truth, this entire network of miners perform the transfers on the blockchain instead of a private server. Because of this factor, the blockchain has really value propositions that I want to highlight here.

"First, transparency. Blockchains are public and open source. Everything that lives on a blockchain is public, and the code that's running the blockchain and the code that applications are using to build on the blockchain are all open-source.

"The second component is this idea of interoperability. I know that's kind of a big scary word but what it really means is the ability to move between applications.

"The third component is that blockchains are immutable. They can't be changed, and this has to do with the decentralized network. You cannot change them once they have been mined." Rex continued, joking, "So growing up, my mom told me—be careful what you put on Facebook, but today we should be saying to our kids, be careful what you place on the blockchain.

"The last thing is that blockchains are programmable. You can create whatever you want. People are building incredible applications on it.

"It's a really key component to understand as you're diving into the space. Thanks for taking the plunge—I know it can be difficult to grasp at first. Did my analogies help?" Rex asked.

"They sure did," Greg, the resident techie, said. "I think the other example that might help the team on blockchain is the ledger example. Do you mind. Rex, if I jump into that discussion too?" Greg was excited to share his expertise in this space too. Given he would be asked to drive technical decisions for their chosen project, he wanted to see how his approach worked with the rabbit team.

"Go for it," said Rex; he was excited to see the team explaining concepts to each other.

"If the storage example was too abstract, I always use the ledger analogy. So a blockchain is a digital ledger. Think about a traditional ledger. What is it used for?" Greg asked, clearly going into teacher mode.

"Well, I know that answer," sang Melissa. "From my MBA days, a ledger is used to record financial transactions, hopefully in a tamperproof way!"

"Yes!" cheered Greg. "So a blockchain is a digital ledger that is used to record transactions digitally. In the same way that a traditional ledger is used to record transactions in a permanent and 'tamperproof way'—using your language, a blockchain uses a decentralized network of computers to record transactions in a secure and transparent manner."

Now Greg stood to draw on the board.

"Each transaction is recorded as a 'block' in the chain, and once it has been added to the chain, it cannot be altered or deleted. This makes blockchain technology particularly valuable for anything that needs to be secure and transparent, such as financial transactions or supply chain management. The decentralized nature of the technology also means that it is not controlled by a single entity, making it resistant to your 'tampering' or fraud."

Greg sat down, pleased with himself as the group applauded.

"Excellent job, Greg!" said Rex as he gave thumbs-up both to Greg and V, who seemed very pleased with the entire interaction.

Rex continued excitedly. "Blockchains are also used to create smart contracts. A smart contract is a self-executing contract—meaning that the terms of the agreement between buyer and seller are directly written into lines of code. Smart contracts are based on blockchain technology and are stored and replicated on a blockchain network.

"How do they work? Well, a smart contract contains a set of rules and penalties that are written in code and stored on the blockchain. Once the terms of the contract are met, the contract automatically executes itself. This allows for the automation of processes and the removal of intermediaries, which can help to reduce costs and improve efficiency. Pretty cool, right? It's a coded contract that is monitored by code!"

Rex paused to see if there were questions. He was a big fan of smart contracts.

"I really love this concept of the smart contract," said Greg. "That means that it would be difficult to alter or manipulate the terms, right? So, the integrity and security of the agreement is stronger?"

"Exactly," Rex replied. "It's one of the reasons that I am a big fan of smart contracts. They allow for the creation of that trustless and tamperproof agreement. In addition, they automate the process and at the same time, remove intermediaries! Everything is encoded into the blockchain!"

A hand went up.

"Trustless?" asked Emma. "That doesn't sound good. I would think you'd want someone who trusted more, right?"

Given Emma's depth of marketing from Reddit, Microsoft, and Nike, she was always thinking about word choice and what you really needed to review to a potential customer.

"I know that this one is hard. It was hard for me to grasp at first too," answered Rex. "Trustless is a term often used in the context of blockchain. It means that the system does not rely on any central authority to function. So, the system can function and be trusted without the need for any specific person or organization to oversee or control it. Instead, trust is placed in the code and the network, which are transparent and tamperproof. Hence trustless.

"Let me give you an example. In a bank that you use today, you need to trust that the bank will keep your money safe right? In a blockchain-based decentralized finance (DeFi) platform, the trust is placed in the code and the network, where the smart contracts that govern the platform are transparent and tamperproof, and the funds are secured by the decentralized network of users."

"What's the business outcome?" asked Emma.

"Great question," Rex praised. "It helps reduce costs and improve efficiency, especially in industries where intermediaries are currently needed to facilitate agreements and transactions. Smart contracts are considered successful in many areas and have been applied in different fields such as finance, supply chain management, and more.

"And remember when we discussed DeFi? The use of smart contracts allows for the creation of decentralized and trustless financial systems, which can help to reduce costs and improve access to financial services for users. In summary, smart contracts are self-executing contracts based on blockchain technology that allow for the creation of trustless and tamperproof agreements, automation of processes, and removal of intermediaries. They have been successfully applied in various fields and have the potential to revolutionize the way agreements and transactions are made."

And with that, the group left for a cookie and coffee break! V had planned for some Austin specials.

She was often quoted as saying, "Coffee is the fundamental fuel that Austinites run on!"

She considered it a necessity for work, study, and play! Her favorite was Crestview's Coffee.

Crestview coffee shop served an array of drinks, and she brought in espresso drinks for her team, including a chocolate–orange blossom latte, iced coffees, matcha, and chai.

Next, she ordered her favorite cookies. Cookies were the spice of life! An Austin institution, Upper Crust's old-fashioned cookies had stood the test of time, so she made sure the chewy, buttery chocolate chip ones would be on hand.

"Having a tasty snack helps the team stay focused and energized while they are learning," thought V.

"Great choices, V," said Rex, munching away. "Did you guys know that there are virtual coffee shops in the metaverse? VR Chat and AltspaceVR allow users to visit virtual spaces and socialize with each other in virtual coffee shops and virtual bakeries."

They all laughed. Was everything Web3, the Metaverse or AI to Rex?!

It didn't matter. Emma and Greg were coffee fiends and dove straight into the delicious coffee blends, experimenting as they went along. Dawn, Tommy, and Johnny went for the cookies, especially the chocolate chip ones.

Johnny commented, "These amazing sweets will help us through digital identity. This is a subject that really peaks my interest as the product manager."

Web3 and Digital Identity

Rex continued the session by moving to the next layer up: Web3.

"Okay, are you guys now ready to move off the backbone and into another interesting layer? Web3 is about digital identity and being able to access those decentralization services. Shall we continue?" he said excitedly.

"WEB3 IS NOT A MOMENT. IT'S A MOVEMENT. AND YOUR WEB3 DIGITAL IDENTITY IS YOUR HUMAN RIGHT."

—Sandy Carter

You could tell how much this subject excited him, and it was contagious. The whole group leaned in to listen to the next section—especially after having sugar and caffeine!

A hand shot up.

Dawn asked curiously, "So, before we go further, in one sentence can you explain what Web3 is? And is it the same thing as the new internet?"

Again, Dawn wanted to make sure that their customer would get these concepts when needed. The answers would guide her on the education plan.

"Sure," said Rex. "Let me start with this definition and then we will break it apart.

"The definition that I like to use is that Web3 is an open movement to broadly decentralize the internet, allowing for ownership of data and digital identity."

He paused for a moment, allowing for the words to sink in.

"So, when we start with an open movement that refers to a broad philosophy that advocates for the open sharing of information and the use of open standards and open-source technologies. This movement is based on the idea that information should be freely available to everyone and that technology should be developed in a way that allows anyone to access and modify it."

Rex stopped his lecture as he saw a hand go up.

"So why do that? There are lots of companies that develop software on their own, right? Is that not a good model?" inquired Johnny, still drawing concepts for product management on his trusted sheet of paper.

"Well, it's not a question of good or bad," answered Rex. "It's a different way to develop or work. Proponents of the open movement believe that open-source technologies are more secure, more transparent, and more innovative than proprietary technologies and that they can lead to more collaboration and faster progress in the tech industry. The open-source software movement has played a significant role in the development of many popular software programs, including the Linux operating system, the Apache web server, and the Mozilla Firefox web browser."

Rex asked if there were any more questions, and no one raised their hand.

"Okay, if that is clear, let's break now the next part: broadly decentralize the internet. We learned that decentralization means that data are not being held by a single central authority. In a centralized system, a single entity has control over the entire system. In other words, it makes the internet more inclusive and more transparent. It can also allow for more equitable distribution of power and resources. And that can enable greater participation and collaboration among all members of a community or system."

Again, Rex paused.

"And that's why it's built on the blockchain, right?" probed Emma, marketer extraordinaire. "The 'decentral-ness' comes from the blockchain, and Web3 makes use of that so that we can access that data, or resources."

Rex jumped about 2 feet in the air!

"That's right, Emma! You are a fast learner. That's why blockchain is the backbone of the whole system. If we continue through the definition, we see that the goal of Web3 is to allow for ownership of data and digital identity.

"First, let's think about digital identity in our current world. "You sign into an application with your identity—or your username and password. And when you sign into that application, all the data from that experience stays with the application. That's why when you then go and sign into another application, you must start all over with your reputation because data are not shared among the applications—it is owned by the application.

"In the Web3 world, that identity and that data are yours—you own that data and that data stay with you. The promise of Web3 is that self-sovereign identity is inevitable. Everyone will own their identity. It will travel with you, meaning that you can take your digital identity and use to sign into numerous applications."

Rex paused when he saw two hands raised.

"Does that mean I could use my digital identity to log into a finance app or a game? I mean the same digital identity?" asked Greg. Greg had studied some of the OpenId standards. OpenID is an open standard and decentralized authentication protocol that allows you to use an existing account to sign into multiple websites, without needing to create new passwords.

"Yes, that's exactly what it means," responded Rex. "And more importantly, the data from that application or game is yours too. So, a big company that owns that application cannot sell your data. The only way someone could look at it would be with your consent. Let that sink in."

Melissa had already started thinking about a strategic implication of this new technology for EdgyMaven.

"So, I, as a person," she asked, "might get a reward from a retailer if it wanted to know that I wear a size 8 shoe or that I just bought a house. And I share the data only if I want to, right?

Nodding, Rex answered, "Yes, that's right. A company now must entice you, the person, to share the data. They no longer buy your data from a large corporation or entity. The rewards go to you. But there is a bigger data solution as well. What are some other ideas of types of data you'd get value out of storing?" asked Rex.

"How about your diploma or your college transcript?" Greg posed. "What if it lived in your digital identity? Since the backbone is the blockchain that means it's secure and immutable so you couldn't fake it! That would have saved me days of time getting my transcript over so that I could get my first job," he joked. "So that record of your graduation could live in your digital identity to demonstrate that you graduated and have a diploma or a certification."

"Oh! I have a potential example, I think," Emma offered. "What about medical records? A friend of mine broke her leg in Brazil and had to have surgery. It took over eight hours to get the right information down to Brazil. If she had that data in her digital identity, she could have given that to them directly. Would that be an example?"

"Yes, yes, and yes," said Rex. "All of these are great examples. Let your imagination run wild here. For example, if EdgyMaven could entice potential customers to provide information on how many certs they had in certain tech and their badges of use in other applications, could that qualify for a reward or a VIP seat at your next event? The possibilities could be endless!"

V had to pause them for a second before they started brain-storming too fast!

"I think we have more layers to get through, right, Rex?" she teased.

"Yes, you are right, V. Let me summarize digital identity before we move on," Rex reiterated. "Digital identity is how your business is known online. In the Web2 world, that's a mix of your website, social media presence, and information about your company online.

"Web3 domains are a new tool for digital identity and the best that has been developed yet. Unlike regular domain names or social media accounts, Web3 domains are decentralized and can only be managed by the owner. This means that when a business invests in securing a Web3 domain as their digital identity, no third party can unilaterally lock them out or shut it down.

"So what can you use it for? Various types of information can be connected to a digital identity, whether it's different crypto addresses, social media profiles, or other off-chain information. This is how your Web3 domain is the foundation of your digital identity. In addition to being able to host a Web3 website directly on your Web3 domain, you can also integrate it into different Web3 apps. There is so much power for an individual and a company in owning their digital identity.

"Before we move on and tackle more, let me discuss an example with blockchain, Web3 digital identity, and the creator economy: NFTs. Let's break down NFT since it is a great example as part of the creator economy."

Non-fungible Tokens (NFTs)

"First, NF stands for non-fungible. Non-fungible is equivalent to assets that are valued differently based on their unique attributes and scarcity (versus fungible, which means the asset can be traded at 1:1 value, like the US dollar). The baseball cards in your attic are non-fungible as would be your Chanel purse or Hummel figurines. With me so far?" asked Rex. When everyone nodded yes, he continued.

"UTILITY IS GREATER THAN HYPE."

—*Sandy Carter*

"T stands for token," he said. "A token is essentially a digital asset. Typically, it is blockchain-based and represents a unique asset like a piece of art, digital content, or media. If we put it all together," Rex motioned like a conductor placing together the melody and harmony of a symphony, "NFTs are like collectibles, only in a digital form. They are verifiable, unique, and therefore scarce, and transferable. Essentially, since NFTs are minted on blockchain, one can easily determine or verify the origin and the current owner of the asset in question in seconds."

"But why are they important?" asked Dawn. "If they're like collectibles in the real world, like a baseball card or a purse, they would be interesting."

"Great question," said Rex. "NFTs are important because they can easily verify assets that can otherwise be sold as fraud. Linking this back to the creator economy, they directly connect artists with their audience. There is no middleman. For instance, I was listening to Ashanti, and she got pennies on the dollar for her Grammy awarded album because agents, studios, and more had to get paid. Now she can turn her songs into NFTs so she can connect directly with her audience while simplifying the transaction as well."

"That sounds almost too good to be true," commented Emma. "What's the downside?"

"Well," continued Rex thoughtfully, "we are in the early stages due to the current state of technological advancement. In addition, regulatory and legal implications are not fully implemented yet, and that education that I know Dawn is interested in isn't there yet.

"Eventually, better technology will be built out, regulations and rules around NFTs will be clearer, and education around this technology will be more available or not even needed as much due to simplified user experience. As blockchain technologies continue to be adopted by enterprise organizations, governments, gaming studios, financial platforms, and more, NFTs will start to play a larger role in our lives and without you even knowing about it. In other words, the tech will become invisible."

"What do you mean by that? How will they become more important and invisible at the same time?" Emma asked.

"NFTs, like art and music, will have their place, but there'll come a time where they'll fade comparatively," Rex theorized. "And here is where I think the opportunity for EdgyMaven comes in. Art and music will be out shone by 'utility' NFTs. What does that mean? NFTs that offer utility to customers with tailored benefits will be the biggest portion of this market."

"Can you provide us an example?" asked Greg.

"Sure, let's look at what Starbucks is doing today," Rex answered. "Starbucks Odyssey is the coffee chain's first foray into building with Web3 technology. The new experience combines the company's successful Starbucks Rewards loyalty program with an NFT platform, allowing its customers to both earn and purchase digital assets that unlock exclusive experiences and rewards. Today, customers earn 'stars,' which can be exchanged for perks, like free drinks. In the Web3 world, its most loyal customers will earn a broader set of rewards while also building community. The NFTs are the passes that allow access to this digital community. So this becomes the NFT gateway for accessing consumers."

"So, in essence," Tommy summarized, "Web2 gatekeeps loyalty and confines you to redeeming within their walled gardens.

Web3 empowers users through choice and enables selling to the highest bidder. Today, it might not matter, but with increased adoption, consumers will begin to demand more. Today all the burden is on the user to find their email for their discount, as well as downloading an application or scanning a QR code."

"And if I continue with your thread, Tommy," proposed Rex, "what do modern consumers demand more than anything else? Convenience. NFTs remove this need for a frontend and most importantly they eliminate responsibility from the user. Imagine ordering your coffee and just providing a wallet address. It's scanned automatically, and you're eligible for 20% off, due to loyalty tokens you own. Web3 domains turn these addresses into human-readable names. This simplicity makes me bullish on digital identity by association. So you can build online reputation from acquiring tokens or NFTs."

"This is totally rad," commented Dawn. "So, people will go about their daily lives and accrue various tokens over time. It won't be long before we are providing Web3 domains at retailers. And maybe even badges for achievements, NFT tickets for sporting events with rewards, and avatars. The future is ours for the making."

Both Rex and V felt like standing with applause! The team was catching on to the power of Web3.

"Oh yes," said Rex. "But first we must go through the final layers: metaverse and DAOs and AI. Then on to use cases before we plan out our strategy. Sorry I got caught up there because the possibilities are endless. Any other questions on Web3 and digital identity?"

No one raised a hand.

"THE METAVERSE IS NOT JUST A VIRTUAL SPACE, IT'S A LIMITLESS CANVAS WHERE CREATIVITY AND INNOVATION CAN THRIVE. IT HAS THE POTENTIAL TO REVOLUTIONIZE HOW WE LIVE, WORK, AND PLAY BY CREATING NEW WORLDS—BOTH CONSUMER AND INDUSTRIAL—WHERE OUR IMAGINATIONS CAN RUN WILD AND OUR DREAMS CAN BECOME REALITY."

—Sandy Carter

The Metaverse

"What is the metaverse?" asked Rex.

Emma gently raised her hand into the air. "A fictional place. Like that movie *Ready Player One?*" That brought the room into laughter!

"Well, it is like *Ready Player One*, except that it is real, and over time will become even more important," explained Rex. "Usually when someone says 'the metaverse,' they are thinking about a 3D digital world where people work, play, and sleep. They experience the melding of the physical and virtual world in a way that feels real and permanent. To me, *the simplest definition is the internet in 3D.*

"The metaverse is a virtual shared space or a digital world. It is a universe that is built on top of Web3 and the blockchain, and it allows users to interact with each other and with digital objects and environments in real time. These digital objects are important. For example, this year, many young people are seeking Roblox digital currency, Robux, as their gift—not cash. It's clear that digital assets are important for this next generation.

"And yes, the concept of the metaverse has been around for decades, but it has gained a lot of attention and hype too in recent years due to advances in technology, particularly in the fields of virtual and augmented reality. These developments have made it possible for users to experience the metaverse in a more immersive and realistic way," Rex finished.

Greg, their technologist, jumped in. "The metaverse is not just a single virtual world, but rather a network of interconnected virtual environments. Some argue that just as we say 'the internet' and not the 'internets,' we should always say 'the metaverse,' which has multiple parts to it. Right?"

"Right as rain," Rex agreed. "These parts can range from simple chat rooms and forums to highly detailed and interactive virtual worlds. Users can access the metaverse using a variety of devices, including computers, smartphones, and specialized virtual reality headsets.

"One of the key features of the metaverse is its ability to support real-time interaction among users. This allows for a wide range of social and economic activities to take place within the virtual world, from gaming and entertainment to commerce and education."

"One of those activities is dating too," Johnny interjected. "I read an article about it."

Johnny had been doing his homework on use cases because his role as product manager would be to ensure that the requirements were customer obsessed and for that to happen, he had to dive deep into as many use cases as he could find.

"Right again," said Rex. "One-third of singles are ready to date in the metaverse according to a new survey from Dating.com. It says the metaverse can help propel dating into the future, especially as AI become more reflective of users.

"And the potential uses and applications of the metaverse are almost limitless. It has the potential to revolutionize many aspects of our lives, from how we communicate and socialize, to how we work and learn. Some experts even predict that the metaverse will become a fundamental part of our daily lives in the future, just as the internet is today."

Tommy raised his hand and asked, "I just read an article that said the 'metaverse is coming out of the basement and into the boardroom.' What does that really mean?"

"Well," Rex responded, "it means that the concepts of the metaverse, which were built on a lot of gaming concepts, like play to earn, leaderboards, and learn to earn, are all becoming part of the strategy of businesses as well.

"For example, Nike bought a virtual shoe company—RTFKT—that enabled them to attract younger buyers as they sold sneakers as NFTs in the metaverse. Their customers could buy a virtual sneaker and wear it, improving its customer experience dramatically, and it gave them brand recognition for a younger crowd. Why did they buy the company? This is just one signal that Nike sees enormous potential in the metaverse.

"As the Nike CEO John Danahoe said: 'This acquisition is another step that accelerates Nike's digital transformation and allows us to serve athletes and creators at the intersection of sport, creativity, gaming, and culture.'

"And then Nike's new physical shoes launch combined virtual reality, augmented reality, and Web3 NFTs. The new Nike RTFKT 'Artifact' sneakers are on sale today, and they feature auto-lacing technology, gesture control, walk detection, lighting segments, connectivity to an application, and wireless charging.

"But that's not all." Rex's excitement started showing. "You can virtually try them on. Their use of augmented reality and AI allows customers to see how their shoes would look in the real world, using their smartphones or other devices.

"And we've mentioned rewards a few times. Using Web3 technologies, NFT ownership signifies the perks to purchase a real shoe. This enables potential access to limited-edition releases and enables product verification to potentially eliminate fake shoes. And on the business side, since there is significant data being generated, the data can help identity a trove of information about the most passionate users, and how they interact with the product and within their on-chain network."

"But," asked Melissa, "isn't this not just metaverse but metaverse combined with the real world?"

"Yes, for sure," Rex agreed. "Companies will continue to blur the lines between physical, virtual, and hybrid products and experiences to find the mix needed as many workers are now working from home, and the younger generations are nearly all virtual. Digital penetrates every aspect of their lives."

V piped in. "My son recently asked me about a Nike shoe. And I was curious and wondered how he knew about the brand at 9 years old. He had never paid attention to any brand before. My son told me, 'I saw them in the metaverse. They have super RAD shoes.' It is a whole new way to introduce brands to this next generation," she finished out her thought with an upbeat tone.

The room was silent. They really hadn't realized how real this space was before.

And so, with complete attention in the room, Rex continued, "Did you know that 70% of blockchain gamers look forward to hanging out with other people in game per Soocial.com, and 75% of 13- to 39-year-olds play a game that brings them into a virtual world—the metaverse per Ypulse? And finally, that 68% of people say their avatar represents part of them, per Contagious.com?"

"Could you pause and define avatar?" asked Johnny. "I just went to see that movie—which was amazing by the way—but is that what you mean by avatar?"

"An avatar is a digital representation of a person for use in a game, metaverse, or digital universe. Some people like their avatars to look like them, and others like them to look like who they'd really like to be. Which would you choose?" Rex asked his audience.

As they sat pondering that question, Dawn chimed in, "I've been creating avatars with Lensa, an AI tool, but they are just for posting. Are there other tools creating avatars for other uses as well?"

"Yes, you can use a few different programs to create an avatar like ReadyPlayerMe and Epic's Unreal Engine." Rex paused to see if there were any other questions. The topic of the metaverse seemed to intrigue more people than just the technology, probably because this was more of an interface layer on top of Web3 and the blockchain.

Tommy raised his hand. "I love playing with avatars in my gaming. Is an avatar in the metaverse the same as that in a game?"

Rex thought for a moment and then answered, "Yea, I guess you can say that it is similar to an avatar in a game. An avatar in a game is simply the player controlled by the user. However, think back to our discussion of digital identity. In the metaverse, the character is a more consistent aspect of the user's identity, and in fact, his or her experiences. And with work being done by groups like the Open Metaverse Alliance or OMA3, that avatar could be used across multiple metaverses. So, I would say an avatar in the metaverse is more expansive."

Rex decided to continue with the metaverse discussion.

"According to Citi GPS, the metaverse is about more than just games and will have five billion users and a $13 trillion market cap by 2030. Some people see the metaverse as a potential replacement for the physical world, offering new ways for people to work, play, and socialize. In fact, you could get a job today in the metaverse. Now I didn't say on the metaverse or about the metaverse, but *in* the metaverse. Some of the top jobs are things like explore or tour guides, lecturers, or event managers for events that take place in the metaverse. Some jobs are just emerging, like security or police or even digital fashion advisors."

"A friend of mine went to the Decentraland Fashion show," Emma said. "And to dress she hired a digital fashion advisor to help her select her earrings, dress, and shoes for the event."

"Yes, and I've read a bunch of articles on tech for good," Dawn added. "For example, doctors and surgeons use it to train others or for education. I've even seen it being used for mental health for the elderly. Many of them said that they aren't limited by physical disabilities in the metaverse. I know the development of the metaverse is still in its early stages, and it is not yet clear how it will evolve. However, it has the potential to revolutionize how we interact with each other and with the world around us especially with AI."

And on that the team was silent. It appeared to V that the team might have some ways that they could not only pursue profit for the company, but purpose as well.

Rex concluded the metaverse section.

"The metaverse gives us unlimited possibilities. The technology—virtual reality, artificial intelligence, and other technologies—allows us work, create, communicate, evolve, travel, and so much more—and all this in whole new digital worlds and dimensions. And avatars can help us build a new us and become who we want to be all the while protecting our digital identity.

"But we must also remember that the metaverse has some challenges too, like spending time with real-world connections. One of the new job roles that have come to be is a chief wellness metaverse officer. If we use the metaverse to replace family and friends, we may run into other issues.

"Let's go back to Emma's comment on *Ready Player One*. That's why the Oasis was closed on Tuesdays and Thursdays. Though the metaverse with all its benefits is awesome and I sincerely believe in it, we still shouldn't forget about our real life," and with that Rex closed out the metaverse layer.

Decentralized Autonomous Organizations (DAOs)

"Okay," observed Rex. "Our final layer of our picture is the DAO. DAO stands for decentralized autonomous organization. With that many syllables, it's obvious why everyone just says DAO instead! But that definition really raises more questions than it answers.

"DAOs ARE HERE TO GIVE POWER BACK TO THE PEOPLE. DECENTRALIZED DECISION-MAKING AND TRANSPARENT GOVERNANCE ARE THE NEW KIDS ON THE BLOCK, AND THEY'RE NOT GOING ANYWHERE ANYTIME SOON."

—Sandy Carter

"So, let's break it down word by word. First, we have decentralized. DAOs are decentralized in two ways: the authority of the group is distributed among the members, and the DAO is built upon a blockchain, which itself is a decentralized network."

As he continued, he saw lots of note taking. This subject was a little bit harder concept to grasp.

"Autonomous also has multiple definitions that apply to a DAO. On one hand, it means that the group is self-governing. It can also refer to the method in which decisions are made. Some DAOs have rules written into the smart contract, which operate without much human oversight.

"And finally, the last word, organization, is the most self-explanatory," teasing he adding, "although some DAOs are seriously lacking in organization."

"So then what's the point of a DAO?" queried Melissa. "Why would someone want to join one?"

"Well," Rex explained patiently, "DAOs have become one of the easiest ways for people to organize around a specific goal or cause or to add an element of user control over a project. Many DAOs distribute governance tokens to their members, which represent their financial and voting rights.

"First up is the Flamingo DAO, one of the most famous and well-funded NFT-focused DAOs. Flamingo DAO is made up of a maximum of 100 members. Becoming a member requires buying a minimum of 100,000 Flamingo Units, which don't come cheap. This entrance fee goes into the DAO's treasury and is used to purchase NFTs. Putting together a group of investors like this has allowed Flamingo DAO to amass one of the most valuable NFT collections in the world, with pieces ranging from generative art to high-end avatars, also known as pfps, or profile pictures.

"DAOs are for more than just buying things—they can also be used to help run an organization. Uniswap is one of the largest decentralized financial networks in the world, allowing people to exchange different types of cryptocurrencies. Uniswap recently introduced its own protocol token, called UNI. The tokens were split, with 60% going to community members, approximately 21% to the Uniswap team, roughly18% to investors, and the last bit for advisors. With the majority going to the community, this was Uniswap's way of rewarding its early supporters and involving them in the future growth of the organization. Holding the tokens allows people to collect part of the fees generated by Uniswap and to vote on how the company is run. If you only want to collect the fees but don't want the stress of voting on proposals, in many DAOs you can delegate your votes to another member.

"Here are a few more examples. The MakerDAO was the first DAO that I learned about. Created in 2014 and credited as the earliest decentralized finance application (defi) to gain real adoption, MakerDAO was created to make a less volatile currency for crypto transactions. Without getting too deep into the financial details, MakerDAO allows people to deposit other collateral like Ethereum or Bitcoin and generate Dai— the stablecoin managed by the Maker Protocol.

"People who own the governance token for MakerDAO, MKR, are able to vote on key decisions for the Protocol, such as the savings rate (number of DAI generated for depositing assets)."

Rex sighed as he thought he might losing some folks, but he pushed on.

"The Blocks DAO is a new type of DAO that is building a platform to help traditional businesses incorporate DAOs. Since it is still a relatively new structure, DAOs can be tricky for IRL (in real life) businesses to adopt. Blocks DAO created a DAO to solve this problem which is very meta: a DAO made to help DAOs."

Dawn raised her hand. "I heard about this group that was trying to buy the Constitution. Was that a DAO?"

Rex grinned. "Yes, it was a DAO. Not all DAOs have long-term goals. Sometimes they can be created for a singular purpose. When a copy of the constitution went on sale (an actual copy of the US Constitution), a group of people online decided they wanted to try to buy it. They created a DAO and raised $40 million dollars from thousands of people in seven days. While they didn't end up winning the auction, it still showed the power of DAOs to help organize people around a common goal.

"But I think DAOs will play an important role in the future of Web3 and the metaverse. Looking to the future of DAOs, they don't have to only be used for these larger organizations. I was listening to Twitter Space with Sandy Carter from Unstoppable, and Kelly Cambry from Blue Studios. Sandy was talking about her family meetings that she holds once a month. In many ways a family is like a DAO, minus the blockchain part. Imagine if your family could put proposals to vote and use some of the same mechanisms of these larger DAOs. So Kelly pulled together a template for a family DAO!

"And who knows where this will go?" shrugged Rex. "Maybe there will be homeowners' associations that incorporate DAOs. What if an entire city or country was run by a DAO? Decentraland—the company I mentioned earlier that hosted a fashion show—is run by a DAO.

"Who knows how far this technology can go, but that is one of the most exciting things about being in the space. We're so early it's like we're the pioneers of the Wild West. These new technologies that we are exploring could one day support whole cities' worth of growth.

"Let's finish up with a few words about AI tools and then we will be done for the week."

Artificial Intelligence (AI)

"I'm going to touch on AI as a set of tools for business leaders. The introduction of AI in the business world has given companies the ability to gain competitive advantages over their competitors. AI provides valuable insights into consumer behavior, purchasing habits, interests, and more, allowing businesses to inform their marketing and product campaigns, improve the customer experience, and gain market insights," Rex began.

"For us, in the Web3 and metaverse space, I think the potential is to use these tools in designing video and images, for copywriting and editing, content creation, and even helping to build metaverse guides. In your week of play, you will be trying out some of the best tools out there right now. And I say right now, as this space is moving quickly.

"I was listening to CNN the other day, and the two biggest technology companies mentioned AI over 75 times among them in their earnings reports!" Rex chuckled. "The point is what I will give you now will be quickly changing; however, the concept of using AI tools to help you be more effective is not.

"For example, generative AI, such as ChatGPT and Dall-E, has the potential to revolutionize content creation. They produce a wide range of content, including audio, code, images, text, simulations, and videos. Companies can benefit from using generative AI to produce clear written materials, technical materials, and more. However, developing a generative AI model is resource-intensive and only feasible for larger companies. Companies can use preexisting generative AI models to benefit from its capabilities," Rex explained.

"Fascinating," Greg commented. "So we will be trying out these as tools to help us in all our areas of marketing, strategy, tech, metaverse and avatar design, and more?"

"That's right," Rex answered. "When used as tooling to help this rabbit team, AI can greatly improve efficiency, accuracy, and productivity. These tools can process large amounts of data faster and more accurately than we mere humans and therefore can process data faster, reducing the risk of errors and freeing up time for us to focus on more complex and creative tasks. That should allow us to focus on more strategic tasks.

"I also believe that AI can provide new insights and decision-making support. One CEO told me he used ChatGPT to create his key performance indicators (KPIs). But first he wrote his own out. He told me the combination was the right set of KPIs for his startup!"

"Okay, I think I get it now," mused Melissa. "Overall, using AI as tools will us increased efficiency, accuracy, and productivity, as well as potentially come up with new opportunities for growth and innovation."

V jumped in. "I like to say that AI augments our intelligence. Hence, I call it augmented intelligence. It isn't replacing our creative intelligence but helping us."

"I love that V. Augmented intelligence!" Rex smiled. "So I'll give you some of the tools that you will use during your play week but remember, this is just a starter set. There are many more coming to be sure.

"For example, for video and image generation, your rabbit team will explore Dall-E, Midjourney, Runway, Jasper Art, and Descript. Some of you will prefer some tools over others, just like in today's world where some love Zoom and others Google Meet."

"And for copywriting and editing, you will try ChatGPT, Jasper, Writer, Hyperwrite, and Cohere. Oh, and by the way, as you create your plan, you may determine you need an AI tool to help in a new area! Search away for those tools. This section is to really help you know that these tools exist. The people who figure out how to use these tools will be the ones who innovate faster.

"But AI is also crucial for the metaverse, especially the industrial metaverse. The industrial metaverse is the next phase for industrial technology, and digital twins are the building blocks of this virtual world. They offer companies the ability to experiment and model products and processes before committing to anything in the real world. The industrial metaverse isn't only for professionals, as cities such as New York and London use digital twins to crowdsource visions of each city's future. With digital twins, companies can predict and prevent potentially costly failures or service interruptions before they happen. The applications of digital twins are endless, and their impact on engineering, operations, and manufacturing is profound.

Digital twins are virtual replicas of physical products, processes, or systems that are updated continuously in real time. That's why many call them industrial metaverses. They provide a bridge between the real world and digital world, enabling companies to experiment and model their products or processes without building expensive physical prototypes. As such, digital twins promise to become the interface for sensor data arriving from the internet of things, combined with AI analytics and human monitoring. Companies are already using them to model, predict, and improve operations from anywhere in the world using virtual ones. AI is very powerful in Web3 and the metaverse, and we will learn how we as individuals and companies will use it as a valued partner," concluded Rex, closing out the section on AI.

Conclusion

Rex, along with V and the rabbit team were ready for the weekend.

He ended with a few words about the potential of the technology. "So this week has been a comprehensive overview of the rapidly evolving and interconnected fields of blockchain technology, Web3, digital identity, NFTs, the metaverse, DAOs, and AI. These technologies have the potential to revolutionize various industries, from finance and art to governance and society at large. However, they also bring new challenges, including security, privacy, and ethics. As the technology continues to evolve, it will be important to stay informed and proactive in shaping its impact on the world. Think about the concepts over the weekend, and we will start fresh on Monday with use cases for each of these areas."

4 | The Use Cases— Business Outcomes

Utility > Hype

The next section of the education session was about use cases. There was so much hype in this new space that Rex wanted to make sure the team understood the real utility being used today, because he always believed that utility was greater than hype!

Rex began chatting with his "students" before the session started.

"There is tremendous value in use cases. They help show how the theory becomes real through the thought process, steps, and resources that would be used. In addition, use cases can reveal whether the choice of approach and technology is a fit for a specific company, and can even identity potential risks. For example, a use case for a metaverse can demonstrate how it can increase engagement, revenue, and customer satisfaction in the gaming industry."

V then hustled into the room. She was the last to arrive and came in wearing her Argent jacket and jeans. V called out above the team's chatting, "I'm so excited now to hear how other leading-edge companies are leveraging all these cool technology and business models. Should we jump right in or are there any questions from yesterday's session?"

"I have a question," Dawn piped up, trying to add in some techie questions she knew she'd need as the educator of the group. "Are there metaverses that don't use Web3 technology?"

"Yes, there are for sure," Rex said. "In fact, the first metaverse I tried was Second Life. Second Life was a place that I lectured in, sold virtual goods, and even made some real money," laughed Rex. "It was successful in training for some organizations and did gain widespread attention. But Web2 technology has some limitations when compared to Web3, which is built on blockchain technology. Web2 metaverses could not offer the same level of security, ownership, interoperability, and scalability as a Web3 metaverse."

Rex then moved on, reshowing the diagram of the layer cake (Figure 3.1).

"What I would like to do is to run through use cases for each of the following layers: Blockchain, Web3/Digital Identity, metaverse, DAOS and NFTS/AI Tools. And then I'd love to share a few case studies that encompass the 'stack.' I think those examples can be used to help us see the mechanisms, resources, and steps that EdgyMaven could learn from and grow. But remember that there are new case studies coming out every day. Make sure you keep up with them, and even create some from EdgyMaven!"

Blockchain Use Cases

"Let's start with blockchain use cases," Rex said. "Of course, the first use case of blockchain was Crypto. I remember hearing one of the first presentations on Bitcoin at SXSW, a conference on emerging tech and companies, held right here in Austin. Bitcoin (BTC) is a digital currency that is based on blockchain technology. It is considered the most widely used blockchain-based currency and has a large market capitalization.

"I'll do three to four diverse use cases for each layer. Let's start with blockchain. Now this one will be the most technical one, with the others building up to more engagement and sexier business outcomes."

MakerDAO

Pointing to the board, he said, "I want to show how DAOs use and leverage the chain. MakerDAO is a DAO that allows anyone to lend and borrow the cryptocurrency DAI, which is pegged to the US dollar. MakerDAO leverages blockchain technology in several ways to achieve its goal of creating a stable coin. As a reminder, stable coins are usually backed by a fiat currency, like the US dollar, but can also be pegged to physical assets like precious metals, or even other cryptocurrencies." Rex paused. "Everyone with me?"

They all nodded their heads.

"First, it uses smart contracts on the blockchain to automate the process of creating and redeeming DAI. These smart contracts are transparent, tamperproof, and self-executing, making it easy for anyone to participate in the system.

"In addition, MakerDAO uses blockchain technology for transparency and trustlessness. All transactions and activities on the MakerDAO platform are recorded on the Ethereum blockchain, which allows anyone to see and verify the overall stability of the system."

"But what are the business outcomes they get as opposed to using some other tech?" asked Johnny.

Rex replied, "MakerDAO achieves several business outcomes by using blockchain technology, including decentralization, censorship resistance, a stablecoin, smart contracts, and transparency. MakerDAO operates as a DAO, which means that it is a decentralized organization that is run by its community of users on chain. This allows for more transparency and fairness in the decision-making process, and it also helps to reduce the risk of censorship or manipulation.

"Because it's built on the blockchain, it's immutable and transparent, which means that the transactions and data on the platform cannot be altered or deleted by any central authority, making it more resistant to censorship.

"MakerDAO uses smart contracts on the blockchain to automate the process of creating and managing DAI. This helps to reduce the need for intermediaries and increases the efficiency of the system.

"And finally, it's transparent. All the data and transactions are publicly available on the blockchain, which allows for greater transparency and accountability. I know that was a lot of technical information, but I wanted you to see the power of the chain.

"Let's head on to case study 2," said Rex, holding two fingers up in the air.

Ripple

"Cross-border payments is an interesting area to add value to," Rex said. "Ripple is a blockchain-based platform that enables fast and cost-effective cross-border payments. Several banks, including Santander and American Express, have implemented the technology for international money transfer. Ripple, the company behind the XRP cryptocurrency, uses blockchain technology to power its payment protocol and enable fast and low-cost cross-border transactions.

"One of the main reasons why Ripple chose to use blockchain technology is because of its ability to facilitate secure and transparent transactions. Blockchain technology allows for the creation of a tamperproof and transparent digital record of all transactions that occur on the Ripple network. This helps to ensure the integrity and security of the transactions and makes it easy to track and trace payments as they move through the system.

"But that's not the only reason Ripple is using the blockchain. It also allows for the creation of a decentralized network. The Ripple network is not controlled by any single organization or entity, which means that transactions can occur directly between users without the need for intermediaries. This helps to reduce the costs and inefficiencies associated with intermediaries and intermediaries' fees. The blockchain technology is improving speed, cost, and transparency. You will see these value points in each of the case studies."

"What about value for their users?" asked Emma. "I know this is a business-to-business case study, but the users should see value too, right?"

"Right you are," sang Rex. "Utilizing blockchain technology improved the overall experience for users and businesses. American Express has piloted a blockchain-based payment system that allows its corporate customers to make B2B payments to suppliers in real time using a digital ledger. This technology allows American Express to increase the speed, transparency, and security of B2B payments while also reducing the cost of transactions."

"I think I'm seeing the patterns of value for blockchain," said Dawn. "You said you had four examples. Do they all have the same value?"

"Well," started Rex. "This one is in early stages, but I see a lot of potential for it. What is it? Real estate."

Propy

With a twinkle in his eye, Rex went on. "Propy is a global real estate platform that uses blockchain to facilitate online property purchases and sales. It utilizes smart contracts and its own cryptocurrency to streamline the process of buying and selling property, including deeds and title transfers. The platform allows buyers and sellers to complete transactions entirely online, including the signing of legal documents and transfer of funds, making the process faster, more secure, and more transparent."

"And an exciting development is the use of NFTs as well. Propy developed a feature called 'Propy NFTs.' As a reminder, NFTs are a type of digital asset that can represent ownership or proof of authenticity of a real-world asset, such as a piece of art, collectible, or a real estate property. In the case of Propy, these NFTs are used to represent ownership of a property on the blockchain, making it easy to transfer ownership and track the history of a property in a secure and transparent way."

Rex scanned the team, looking for questions.

"But what about the real estate agenda?" asked Dawn "I know even with Redfin and Zillow, the real estate agent is very important."

"For sure," agreed Rex. "Real estate agents still play an important role in Propy's platform. They can help people navigate the process of buying and selling property, provide market insights, and connect buyers with other parties such as lawyers. However, with the use of smart contracts and blockchain technology, real estate agents can benefit from a more efficient and secure way to handle the transaction process, from listing and showing properties, to signing legal documents and transferring ownership. Propy has successfully used its platform for several pilot transactions, including the purchase of a property in California, which was recorded on the blockchain.

"I must say though that the adoption and use of blockchain technology in the real estate sector is still considered to be in its early stages, with more research, testing, and regulations needed to be created to allow for broader adoption. There are so many exciting and creative things happening in this space. These are just a few examples of how blockchain technology is being used in various industries. There are many more successful case studies in areas such as finance, health care, and government."

California Department of Motor Vehicles (DMV)

"I also want to include a case study of blockchain with the California Department of Motor Vehicles, or DMV," Rex said. "This is just in the early stages, but I wanted to share the thought process for sure!

"The DMV in California plans to use blockchain technology for record keeping, including the issuance of car ownership, and simplifying transfers of such ownership.

"Basically, the DMV will leverage blockchain to serve as a platform for deploying smart contracts. The move is part of a collaboration among the California DMV, Tezos (a type of blockchain), and blockchain software firm Oxhead Alpha. They recently announced the successful completion of a proof-of-concept blockchain-based vehicle titling solution."

"So the business outcomes they're looking for are car ownership titles and transfers?" asked Tommy.

"Yes, let me explain," said Rex. "The blockchain-based system would allow for a secure and decentralized record of car ownership. The chief digital officer at the California DMV, Ajay Gupta, says he hopes the plans to materialize the title database on blockchain come to fruition soon. Following that, the agency also aims to build consumer-facing applications, including digital wallets that hold car title NFTs. This could really improve the process of transferring car ownership."

The class was mesmerized.

"Leveraging blockchain technology," Rex continued, "could help address issues like transaction fraud and tracking the cars' movement. Plus, the use of digital ledgers for generating and transferring car titles is an opportunity for the agency to modernize its processes."

"So, I'm curious." asked Melissa. "Since we will have to select a project or two to start working, do we know why the DMV is focusing on car titles specifically?"

"There are a few reasons," Rex explained. "Car titles today are a painful process. If the DMV evaluated its citizen experience like EdgyMaven does for customer experience, it would choose to focus on one that has room for improvement and could serve as a first beta. Also, car titles are one option that has gained some attention recently. A startup out of Cleveland raised $5 million to digitize car titles, and the state of California published a report the same year identifying possible pilots for blockchain, with the DMV included as one of the options.

"And I think this will be a first case example, where, if it's successful, others will follow suit. Several US congressional representatives have discussed plans to promote a progressive regulatory framework for digital assets to make sure that America is the place for innovation in fintech and blockchain. And in a report earlier this month, the World Economic Forum said it believes blockchain technology will continue to be an 'integral' part of the modern economy. So we may see more and more government agencies exploring the use of blockchain technology in the future."

He looked around the room to make sure everyone was still with him. Everyone in the group was absorbing these use cases. They started to mark up on a whiteboard the power of blockchain and what it could bring to a company.

"Shall we move on to Web3 and digital identity, moving up the layer cake?" asked V. Everyone nodded yes!

Web3 and Digital Identity Use Cases

Rex started the conversation. "Hey, everyone! Today we're going to talk about some of the ways that different companies and governments have used blockchain-based digital identity solutions to improve their operations."

Blockchain.com

You could tell that Rex was excited about this digital identity use case. It was exciting because it was with one of the best companies in the Web3 space.

Rex began: "Let me start with Blockchain.com and tell you a little about who it is and what it does. Blockchain.com is a leading provider of cryptocurrency and blockchain services, including a popular digital wallet and trading platform. It is known for its commitment to security, reliability, and user-friendly interface. It also provides a wide range of educational resources to help users learn about the potential of blockchain technology and how to use it. It is also known for its high-volume trading, with one of the largest Bitcoin trading platforms in the world."

Rex finished his description to turn and see a comment coming from the team.

"It is an impressive company." Emma chimed. "I cannot wait to hear what it did with digital identity. And I'm curious if that was one of the first things they did for their community."

"Blockchain.com partnered with a company called Unstoppable Domains to implement a decentralized identity verification system—or as we've been discussing it—a digital identity. This allowed Unstoppable customers to create and manage their own digital identities on the blockchain, which could then be used to securely and efficiently verify their identities with Blockchain.com."

Now the class was really into the discussion. Questions began to flow more readily!

Tommy remarked, "So what does that mean for the customer during the onboarding process?"

"Well, Tommy," Rex answered, "it means that customers can easily and securely verify their identity using their digital identity on the blockchain. This improves the efficiency of the onboarding process and reduces the risk of fraud and identity theft. Plus, now users own their own data."

"And what are the benefits for Blockchain.com?" asked Dawn.

"For Blockchain.com," Rex explained, "it is able to onboard new customers faster and more securely. It is also able to improve the overall customer experience by simplifying the work required to verify identities."

Melissa was loving these stories. "That sounds like a win–win for both the company and the customer. It's always great when new technology can improve security and efficiency for everyone."

"Exactly, Melissa," said Rex. "And this is just one example of how digital identity is being used in the financial industry. Many other companies are implementing similar solutions, and it will be interesting to see how it evolves in the future."

Bandit Network

"Now let's move to another interesting use case for digital identities on the blockchain. Have any of you heard of the Bandit Network?" Rex asked.

"I have," said Emma. "In my research I found that it was a platform for creating and trading NFTs. Bandit Network allows users to create and trade NFTs. The platform is known for its user-friendly interface, making it easy for creators to mint and sell them."

"Wow! Our whole class is on fire!" Rex exclaimed. "Bandit also recently implemented a unique solution to honor the creators who were the first to make NFTs on their platform. They created a special token called Soul Bound Tokens, or SBTs, to attract these original creators back to the platform.

"That's cool," said the pragmatic Tommy. "But what does it have to do with digital identities?"

Rex laughed. "Along with the creation of the SBTs, Bandit Network also made it possible for users to easily log into the platform using Web3 digital identity. This allows users to own and control their digital identity and data on the platform."

"So," Dawn responded slowly. "The combination of the NFTs, SBTs, and digital identity provided a way for users to prove that they were the first creators on the platform?"

"Exactly, Dawn!" Rex said. He almost hopped to the board. "By using digital identity to log in, original creators can easily prove that they were the first to make NFTs on the Bandit Network. But it's not just for original creators; it makes the experience of using the platform smoother and easier for everyone. And how does it work? Well, the digital identity system is integrated into the login process on the Bandit Network marketplace. So, when users log in, they can use their digital identity to prove their identity and access the platform."

"So," pondered Greg. "It's like a more secure and efficient way to log in compared to traditional methods AND the data are the users. Meaning that the user can get value from having that data."

"Exactly, Greg. By using a digital identity on the blockchain, the process is more secure and less prone to fraud or identity theft. And it also improves the overall user experience by simplifying the process of logging in and the user gets to keep their data, unlike on a Web2 platform where the digital identity is tied to the platform and thus the data are owned by that platform."

As Rex finalized the case study on Bandit, he started on the third use case for digital identity.

Atari

"Now we are moving on to a company all of you know: Atari and its recent venture into the world of Web3," Rex said. "As you know, Atari is an iconic brand in the video game industry, and it wanted to bring that legacy into the digital world. It launched AtariX and a 50th Anniversary NFT collection with graphic designer Butcher Billy to attract both old and new fans to its ecosystem.

"Atari wanted to make it easy for users to onboard to its platform and transact with one another. It partnered with Unstoppable to implement a Web3 digital identity solution, which allows users to own their own data and identity. This makes it easier to transact by using human-readable names instead of long alphanumeric crypto wallet addresses."

"So, you're saying that with Web3 digital identity, it's easier for people to join and use AtariX?" Tommy asked.

"And it's not just AtariX, either, Tommy," Rex answered. "With one universal username, users can transact with hundreds of integrated applications. This makes onboarding fast and simple, which leads to increased user engagement on the platform."

Rex continued to draw on the board, showing the company name and the business outcome it received.

Dawn spoke up. "That's really interesting. I've never thought about how digital identity can make it easier for users to join and use a platform. It makes sense, though. It's like how we use our email addresses to log into different websites."

"Yeah, but with Web3 digital identity, users actually own their own data and identity. It's a big step forward in terms of user privacy and security," Rex said, moving on. "And AtariX saw great success with this implementation. Its NFT collection sold out and hundreds of users claimed their Web3 digital identities. It's exciting to see such a well-known and respected brand like Atari embrace the power of Web3 and reward its users with a seamless experience."

Since Rex had primarily been talking about companies as examples, he again wanted to mix it up and provide an example of a government leveraging the power of digital identity too.

Government of Estonia

"I'd also like to share a government example. Now, I know you are a company," Rex chuckled, "but we can learn from all examples. Let's discuss the implementation of digital identity by the government of Estonia. As many of you may know, Estonia has been a pioneer in the use of digital identity and blockchain technology. It launched a system called e-Estonia, which allows citizens to access a wide range of government services online using a unique digital identity."

"That sounds really convenient," piped up Emma. "Why did the government decide to implement this system?"

"The main reason was to improve the efficiency and convenience of government services for citizens. By allowing citizens to access government services online, the government was able to reduce the need for physical visits to government offices and save time and money. And of course security was top of mind. So how does the digital identity system ensure that only authorized individuals are able to access government services?

"The government of Estonia chose to use blockchain technology to secure the digital identity system. Blockchain technology allows for the creation of a tamperproof and transparent digital record of all transactions and activities that occur in the system. This helps to ensure the integrity and security of the digital identity system."

"Wow, that's really impressive," Dawn said. "Have there been any positive results from the implementation of this system?" She knew that this was not about technology but about the outcomes the technology brings.

"Yes, there have been," explained Rex. "The government has reported that the use of digital identity has helped to reduce the time and costs associated with government services for citizens and has also helped to improve the security and integrity of government services."

Melissa joined in. "I can see how that would be beneficial. Has the Estonian digital identity system been used as a model for other countries?"

"Yes, it has," Rex replied. "The Estonian digital identity system has been used as a model for other countries looking to implement similar systems. Additionally, the Estonian government is constantly looking for ways to improve its digital identity system and has been developing new solutions such as X-road, a decentralized digital identity infrastructure, and KSI blockchain, a blockchain-based system for securing digital identities and digital assets."

"That's really interesting," Greg chimed in. "It's great to see a government taking such a proactive approach to implementing technology for the benefit of its citizens. And leading-edge technology at that."

"Yes, it is," Rex agreed. "And it's important to note that this is just one example of how digital identity and blockchain technology can be used to improve government services. There are many others as well. At Davos in 2023, digital identity was one of the hot topics at the sessions there. There are more examples as well, but I want us to stay focused on our layer cake!" Rex was on a mission to get them through the use cases so that they could focus on EdgyMaven.

Everyone seemed more excited to hear about the metaverse use cases.

"Certainly, the metaverse has captured the attention of many companies due to its potential for immersive experiences and new forms of digital interaction," concluded Rex. "Unlike the traditional internet, the metaverse allows users to create and interact with digital environments in a more realistic and engaging way. This opens a wide range of possibilities for companies, such as creating virtual storefronts, virtual events, and virtual training simulations."

The class had seen earlier in the week that the metaverse also has the potential to generate new revenue streams through virtual goods and services.

So, while the Web3 technologies, blockchain, and smart contracts were interesting, they were still more infrastructure oriented, except for the power of digital identity.

The class looked forward to exploring the potential of the metaverse as a way to differentiate themselves and stay ahead of the curve.

Metaverse Use Cases

For the next section on value in the metaverse, Rex and V decided to switch it up a bit. V set up a fireside chat and quizzed Rex on the business outcomes they could expect from the metaverse.

"Welcome to this fireside chat, where we are joined by our expert on the metaverse, Rex. Yes, I know, just imagine a fireplace sitting in between us!" joked V. "Today, we will be discussing the potential business outcomes of the metaverse and its impact on various industries." V looked down at her notes and asked, "Rex, the metaverse has been making waves in recent times. Can you give us a quick overview of what it is and why it's important?"

"Sure," Rex began. "The metaverse refers to a virtual world where people can interact with each other and digital objects in a fully immersive and interactive way. It has the potential to transform many industries and create new business opportunities."

The class really wanted to dive into this section today, so V continued, "Can you give us a few examples of how the metaverse could impact businesses?

You could see Rex kind of chuckle with their fireside chat setup. But then he fully engaged and began sharing his expertise.

"The metaverse could have a significant impact in the areas of e-commerce, marketing and advertising, virtual training, virtual real estate, gaming, socializing, remote working and collaboration, and virtual entertainment. Companies can create virtual storefronts and marketplaces in the metaverse, allowing customers to browse and purchase goods and services in a more immersive and interactive way. This opens new opportunities for companies to connect with their customers and offer a more personalized shopping experience."

V was on her game and continued to dive deeper. "That's certainly a game changer for e-commerce. What about marketing, advertising, and training?"

"Companies can use the metaverse to create virtual events, product launches, and other marketing campaigns that allow customers to engage with their brand in a more meaningful way," Rex answered. "The immersive and interactive nature of the metaverse offers new opportunities for companies to create unique and engaging marketing experiences.

"Also, I'm seeing a lot of use by universities, consulting companies, and industrial teams using the metaverse to create virtual training simulations that help employees learn new skills and procedures in a more engaging and interactive way. For remote working, companies are creating virtual office spaces where remote employees can work and collaborate in a more realistic and engaging way.

"For the metaverse," he began as he drew on the board, "we see the prime business outcomes around a set of areas. The potential business outcomes of the metaverse are numerous and varied, but there are some key areas where it could have a significant impact."

He shared on his PowerPoint slides to make it easier to comprehend:

- **E-commerce:** Companies could create virtual storefronts and marketplaces in the metaverse, allowing customers to browse and purchase goods and services in a more immersive and interactive way.
- **Marketing and advertising:** Companies could use the metaverse to create virtual events, product launches, and other marketing campaigns that allow customers to engage with their brand in a more meaningful way.
- **Virtual training:** Companies could use the metaverse to create virtual training simulations that help employees learn new skills and procedures in a more engaging and interactive way.
- **Virtual real estate:** Companies could use the metaverse to create and sell virtual land, buildings, and other assets that can be used for a variety of purposes, such as virtual events, virtual offices, and virtual stores.
- **Gaming:** Companies could use the metaverse to create new forms of gaming experiences that are more immersive and interactive, such as virtual reality games and massive multiplayer online games.
- **Socializing:** Companies could use the metaverse to create virtual spaces where people can socialize and interact with each other in a more engaging and immersive way.
- **Remote working and collaboration:** Companies could use the metaverse to create virtual office spaces where remote employees can work and collaborate together in a more realistic and engaging way.

- **Virtual entertainment:** Companies could use the metaverse to create virtual shows, concerts, and other forms of entertainment that allow audiences to immerse in an interactive digital space.

"We won't walk through examples for each of these but know that the metaverse has the potential to transform many industries and to create new business opportunities. Let's explore four examples."

Forever 21

V continued in their "fireside" setup. "I'd love to hear first about what Forever 21 did!"

"This is a great use case," Rex said. "For those of you who don't know, Forever 21 is a retail company that specializes in fast fashion clothing and accessories. Let's start by understanding what Forever 21 wanted to achieve. Forever 21 wanted to increase its engagement with customers. This meant that it wanted a way to form a strong community. A community is a group of people who share common interests, values, and goals. These people come together and interact with each other to pursue their common interests and to support one another. Members of a community work together to achieve common goals, to share resources and information, and to provide each other with support and encouragement. Communities play an important role in helping people connect and form relationships with others who share similar interests."

V commented, "Communities are the lifeblood of Web3 and the metaverse. Explain a bit more, Rex, about Forever 21's goal for this community."

"With a focus on community, Forever 21 aimed to increase brand awareness and loyalty," Rex elaborated. "It understood that these key aspects were built on several factors. First, building an emotional connection with the community was crucial in generating brand loyalty. Personalizing experiences, such as customizing products to meet each customer's unique needs, helped in forming that connection. Additionally, the power of rewards in the metaverse and Web3 couldn't be ignored. Offering exclusive offers, discounts, and incentives helped drive brand loyalty. Finally, Forever 21 strived to offer a transparent, ethical, and trustworthy experience to the community. When executed correctly, this community-centric approach would result in a surge in sales for the company."

The team was impressed with such big goals from the metaverse.

Rex didn't pause long before he continued the Forever 21 story. "What makes Forever 21 different from other retailers is its innovative approach to the metaverse. Forever 21 has created a game called Shop City, which allows players to express their individuality by building and managing their own virtual store within the game. The game features unprecedented customization options and is a community-first game. It showcases the latest trends in fashion and allows players to test out new products and categories with a vast range of avatar merchandise."

Emma raised her hand and then exclaimed, "That sounds cool! How do they promote the game and merchandise? I know it's not 'build it and they will come.'"

"That's a great question, Emma," Rex answered. "Forever 21 uses an innovative marketing strategy called Infinite Loop™, which connects the in-game experience with exclusive merchandise drops and real-life channels, such as social media, e-commerce, store point of sale (POS), fashion influencers, special QR codes, Out of Home, and Times Square jumbotrons.

"Forever 21 has achieved great success in the metaverse, specifically on the Roblox platform. In fact, the brand has now become the number one retail brand on the platform, selling more units than major brands like Nike, Vans, NFL, and Polo Ralph Lauren. It has established itself as a leader in the metaverse retail space on Roblox, and it has changed the way we shop and experience fashion. I hope you found this story interesting and inspiring. Let me summarize this on the board too."

As Rex went to the board, he repeated, "Forever 21's metaverse and Shop City strategies have resulted in several positive outcomes for the business."

On the board, the class saw his summary:

1. Increased engagement with customers: By offering a unique and immersive gaming experience, Forever 21 has been able to increase engagement with its customers and build a strong community of fashion-savvy players.
2. Boosted sales: The Shop City game has resulted in a significant increase in sales for Forever 21. The brand has become the number one retail brand on the Roblox platform, outpacing major brands like Nike, Vans, NFL, and Polo Ralph Lauren.
3. Enhanced brand image: Forever 21's innovative marketing strategies and strong presence in the metaverse have helped to enhance the brand's image and position it as a leader in the retail space.
4. Improved customer loyalty: By offering players unique and exclusive merchandise drops, Forever 21 has been able to increase customer loyalty and build a strong community of fans.

"So for a summary," Rex continued, "here's what I'd say. As the world searches for proof points whether the metaverse can deliver on its promise now or it's just too soon to tell, Forever 21, the global trend fashion brand, provides one of the most impactful use cases that clearly demonstrates the time is now. First it partnered with the Virtual Brand Group, or VBG, who specializes in transforming global brands into metaverse businesses that generate revenue. In VBG's first 12 months working with the brand, it launched one of the most successful fashion experiences on Roblox, built a virtual fashion empire, created Barbie's first ever virtual clothing line, and even won an award for 'Best Digital Product' (besting heavyweights Lego, Marvel, Stranger Things, and Coca-Cola). To cap off the one-year meta-versary, Forever 21 created the world's first in-real-life fashion line that was incubated virtually by VBG and based purely on user-generated content.

"And I love this quote by Justin W. Hochberg, the CEO of Virtual Brand Group. He said, 'The virtual to physical product launch was one of our most successful activations with any brand yet because it weaved together five innovations seamlessly. We delivered: Virtual revenue. Virtual R&D. Empowered the community letting them design the products. Sustainability (testing items virtually has no supply chain issues and no waste). Last it not least merging virtual with real life, which is how gen Z consumers want their experience. This is how it's supposed to work and the new play book for brands going forward in any sector.'"

After he finished writing on the board, Rex concluded, "Overall, Forever 21's metaverse and Shop City strategies have been a huge success for the business, leading to increased engagement, sales, brand image, and customer loyalty."

"Wow that's a great case study, Rex," V exclaimed. "Let's go onto our next one, which is Accenture. Now, where Forever 21 was a great example for a business-to-customer (B2C) company, Accenture is using the metaverse in a business-to-business (B2B) way to onboard its employees and host customer meetings in the metaverse. Let's go deep dive into that example."

Accenture

The energy in the room was palatable. Hearing about all these experiments going on across the globe gave the team hope and empowerment to try some things for EdgyMaven.

Rex began this next case study with a little background.

"Accenture is a global professional services firm that provides consulting, technology, and outsourcing services to a wide range of industries. To onboard new employees effectively and efficiently, the company has begun using the metaverse, a virtual world that allows users to interact with each other in a shared, immersive environment.

"I went into the metaverse training like a new hire." he paused as he thought about how to share that experience with the team. "As I entered the virtual world, I could see the excitement in the eyes of the new hires as they explored the company's culture and values. They were interacting with other employees, participating in virtual events, and building a sense of community.

"I was impressed at how Accenture was delivering training and development opportunities in an interactive and engaging way. New hires participated in virtual simulations and role-playing exercises that were helping them to develop the skills and knowledge they needed to be successful in their roles. I liked how the metaverse allowed employees who were working remotely or in geographically dispersed teams to access training and development opportunities regardless of their location."

Rex then turned his attention to the onboarding process, which was quick and efficient.

Rex explained, "In traditional onboarding processes, employees may need to travel to a central location or wait for in-person training sessions to be scheduled. But in the metaverse, employees could begin the onboarding process immediately and could participate in training and development activities at their own pace. This was helping to reduce the time it took for new hires to become fully productive members of the team.

"Additionally, Accenture is also using the metaverse to host meetings for its customers. The metaverse provides a unique and immersive experience for customers, allowing them to engage with Accenture and its employees in a virtual environment. This can help to foster stronger relationships and provide customers with a more memorable and enjoyable experience. The metaverse also provides a flexible and scalable solution for hosting large meetings, making it possible for Accenture to connect with customers from around the world, regardless of location or time zone.

"In conclusion, Accenture's use of the metaverse has been a major success and has allowed the company to streamline its onboarding process, provide engaging training and development opportunities, and build stronger relationships with customers. The metaverse is a powerful tool that offers a unique and immersive experience, and Accenture's success with it is a testament to its potential to transform the way companies interact with their employees and customers."

Overall, the team was blown away by Accenture's use of the metaverse. They could see how the company was building a sense of community and belonging among new hires, delivering training and development opportunities in an interactive and engaging way, and onboarding employees quickly and efficiently. And then having customer meetings in the metaverse made so much sense. They were all gaining confidence that this was only the beginning of how the metaverse would transform the way companies interact with their employees and customers.

V had the team stop working for a quick break. She had planned for something fun today—an ice cream and soda bar. She thought it would be a unique way to take a 20-minute break with her squad!

"So now for a bit of a break and some fun. You can create your own unique fruit-infused ice cream or soda mocktails using a variety of flavors and toppings. We also have a selection of healthy snacks like popcorn and cookies to complement the drinks."

Her team teased her. "Are cookies really healthy, V?" laughed Emma.

"Well," V said with a soft laugh. "I tried so I ordered oatmeal cookies made with whole grain oats, natural sweeteners like honey and maple syrup, and dried fruit. In addition, I added my favorite peanut butter cookies made with natural peanut butter, almond flour, and coconut sugar. I'd consider that healthy!!!"

The team took a relaxed break in a playful atmosphere with lively music to solidify connection among the members. V was hoping this lighthearted and refreshing time would recharge and boost team morale as they built up to their challenge: to create a best of breed customer experience using Web3, the metaverse, and AI !

BMW

As the team reassembled in the conference room, V and Rex took their places in fireside chat position.

"Let's continue on now with our last two use cases for the metaverse," V said while sipping on her Cherry Coke mocktail from the break. "I think we'd like to hear how BMW is using the metaverse to get closer with its customers."

Rex began with a background on BMW.

"BMW is a German multinational corporation that produces luxury vehicles and motorcycles. It is one of the world's largest producers of premium cars and is headquartered in Munich, Germany. BMW is known for producing high-quality and stylish vehicles, including sedans, SUVs, and sports cars, that are highly sought after by consumers around the world.

"Its goals for the metaverse were around improving the efficiency and speed of its design and development process. It wanted to stay on its innovative top game as well as improve the quality of its cars. Now, BMW is known for its leading use of tech. BMW sought to create a research and development space where engineers, designers, and others could work together to create even better cars and motorbikes.

"BMW's success with the metaverse can be attributed to several factors. First, the company made the wise decision to invest in virtual reality technology, which allowed it to create a metaverse platform that was both realistic and immersive. This allowed engineers, designers, and other employees to work together in a virtual environment, where they could interact with virtual prototypes of new cars and make changes in real time. This collaboration among different departments allowed for a more streamlined and efficient design process, which resulted in reduced costs and a faster time-to-market.

"BMW also made use of the metaverse platform to collect and analyze data. The platform allowed for the visualization of simulation results, which was a huge advantage for the company. These data were used to make decisions about the design and development of new cars, leading to improved quality and performance. The use of the metaverse technology also allowed BMW to test new designs in a more realistic and immersive environment, which was crucial in ensuring that its cars met the high standards that BMW is known for.

"BMW's success with the metaverse can be attributed to its wise investment in virtual reality technology and the use of its metaverse platform for collaboration, data visualization, and testing. The company's use of the metaverse has allowed it to improve the efficiency and speed of its design and development process, which has reduced costs and allowed for faster time-to-market. Additionally, the use of the metaverse has also allowed BMW to improve the quality of its cars and stay at the forefront of innovation in the automotive industry."

V jumped back in. "Another great case study, again with a little different business outcomes to be sure. Now let's do a government example like we have for the rest of the layers, Rex. Korea seems to be on fire for all things Web3 and the metaverse. Do you have a great story to share from Seoul?"

Seoul, South Korea

"Of course!" Rex responded. "Seoul, South Korea, has taken a bold step forward in exploring the possibilities of a metaverse city, aiming to enhance the urban experience for both its residents and visitors. The city had a clear vision for what it wanted to achieve, and it worked hard to bring this vision to life."

"I think I read about this approach from Seoul," chimed in Melissa. "Its strategy was well thought out. What were its major goals?"

"The first goal," explained Rex, "was to increase the city's digital presence and create a virtual space that could be used by residents and visitors. To do this, the city developed a virtual reality platform that would allow users to explore the metaverse city in 3D. The platform was designed to be seamless and accessible, with the aim of attracting a wide range of citizens.

"To make the metaverse city truly special, the city worked with local artists, start-ups, and developers to create a variety of virtual experiences. These experiences included virtual tours, interactive games, and cultural events, all aimed at providing a unique and engaging experience for users.

"And," Rex warned, "the city wanted to make sure it was successful and knew it needed an ecosystem to help it. To ensure the platform was accessible and widely used, the city established partnerships with major tech companies and virtual reality hardware providers. This helped to ensure that the platform was well supported and could reach a wide audience."

"Okay, I've waited long enough," begged Emma. "Tell me how they marketed it."

"Yes," Rex chuckled, "the city invested in marketing and promotion to raise awareness of the metaverse city and attract users. This included promoting the platform through social media and other marketing channels, as well as creating exciting and innovative experiences that would capture people's attention."

Rex stopped to gather his thoughts around the outcomes.

He continued, "The results of these efforts were clear. The metaverse city helped to increase the city's digital presence, giving it a unique and innovative edge. It attracted investment and boosted the city's overall economic competitiveness by offering a new and innovative experience. The platform provided a space for local start-ups and small businesses to showcase their products and services, fostering entrepreneurship and creativity. Finally, the metaverse city brought people together and created a sense of community through shared virtual experiences, improving overall community engagement.

"To summarize, overall, Seoul's metaverse city has been a success, achieving its goals and providing a unique and innovative experience for its residents and visitors. The city's investment in this project has paid off, and it has become a model for other cities looking to embrace the potential of the metaverse."

"Great job, Rex," complimented V. "These case studies are helpful as they spur ideas for us to consider for our opportunities too. So, my summary would include the following key points. First, the metaverse can provide a highly immersive and interactive experience, allowing users to enter and interact with virtual worlds. But it can also help internal teams, especially remote teams, to work together in a shared virtual space, allowing for more efficient collaboration and communication. Since the metaverse is changing the game for commerce and community, we also learned that the metaverse can provide a platform for virtual commerce, allowing users to buy and sell goods and services in a virtual environment. This could include virtual real estate, virtual goods, and virtual services such as design and consulting."

As V continued, the team was taking copious notes.

"Metaverses have the potential to revolutionize the way we form communities, offering a new level of immersive experiences that go beyond what is possible with traditional virtual reality and augmented reality technologies. These immersive spaces have a wide range of potential use cases, from gaming and entertainment to education and commerce."

V wanted to highlight gaming. Not just because of Tommy's references to gaming being the first metaverse but because of the power it brought with gamification in the business world too. Gaming was moving out of the basement and into the board room.

She continued to emphasize this point: "One of the key areas where metaverses are already having an impact is in gaming. Metaverse games allow players to enter virtual worlds where they can explore, play, and interact with others in real time. These games are designed to be highly immersive and engaging, offering players a level of interactivity and social connection that is not possible with traditional games.

"Another important use case for metaverses is in the world of education and training. Metaverses can provide students with hands-on learning experiences that are far more immersive and engaging than traditional lecture-style teaching. This is especially important for subjects like science and engineering, where hands-on learning is essential for understanding complex concepts.

"In the world of commerce, metaverses have the potential to transform the way we shop and purchase goods and services. For example, customers can explore virtual showrooms to see products before making a purchase or attend virtual trade shows to discover new products and connect with vendors. The immersive nature of metaverses makes them ideal for these types of experiences, providing a new level of interaction and engagement that is not possible with traditional e-commerce platforms.

"Finally, metaverses are also having an impact on the world of entertainment. Whether it's watching live concerts, attending virtual film festivals, or exploring virtual theme parks, metaverses provide a new level of immersion and interactivity that is not possible with traditional forms of entertainment. The social and community-focused nature of metaverses also makes them an ideal platform for these types of experiences, allowing users to connect and share experiences with others from around the world."

V knew she was summarizing much longer than normal. But she saw so much potential in the metaverse that she wanted to ensure the team had a solid summary. She and Rex had worked on it the day before so that she could "bring it home," if you would, as kind of a summary with a call to action!

So she concluded in this fashion: "Metaverses have the potential to transform a wide range of industries, offering new and innovative experiences that go beyond what is possible with traditional virtual reality and augmented reality technologies. Whether it's gaming, education, commerce, or entertainment, metaverses have the potential to reshape the way we interact with digital spaces and provide new and exciting opportunities for businesses, educators, and consumers alike. And that means that we have our work cut out for us in deciding where we start our journey!

"We had some fun with our fireside chat style of teaching but now we will switch it up again with Rex leading us in the next step of use cases. You guys ready?"

And the whole team said at once, "YES!"

DAO Use Cases

Rex resumed more of a lecture style for the DAO use cases. DAOs had been formed to have community-driven decisions. The top uses for DAOs that Rex had seen were for the goals of crowdfunding, to raise funds for investments, to govern a project or company, for NFT investing, sometimes for fractionized ownership, and then then finally social DAOs for creating a club-like environment.

"I'd like to share three use cases for DAOs. I don't know if EdgyMaven would want to form a DAO for any of their efforts, but DAOs are very important so I want to ensure that you know what they are from use cases as well."

PizzaDAO

"Let's start first with the Pizza DAO," Rex began. "It's a fun story I heard from the Crypto Business Conference hosted by Michael Stelzner. I would title this a story of community, blockchain, and free pizza!"

With that statement, the team chuckled.

"So let me tell you the story. In a world where big pizza chains dominate the market, independent pizzerias often struggle to compete. PizzaDAO, a group of independent pizzeria owners, set out on a mission to level the playing field. They envisioned a world where independent pizzerias had the same technology, supplier relationships, and financial power as the big chains. And they believed that the key to achieving this goal was through the power of blockchain technology and community ownership.

"In February 2021, PizzaDAO decided to throw a global pizza party to celebrate independent pizzerias. They created an NFT to sell so that they could raise funds for their mission. The launch was a huge success, raising around $500K due to the trust that PizzaDAO had built with its network by promising them a slice of the NFT."

The team was amazed with this cool and simple story. "I want a slice," said Melissa.

"The PizzaDAO community," Rex continued, "was drawn to its sticky and viral motto, 'pizza should be free.' The idea was simple: sell digital pizzas as NFTs and use the proceeds to buy real pizza to give away for free. By promising community members they'd get a token that represents the DAO's mission, they felt a sense of ownership in that mission. And when the DAO was successful in its mission, everyone who held one of those tokens in their wallet had tangible evidence of their part in that success.

"PizzaDAO transformed itself into the 'Federal Reserve of free pizza.' Its token represented the belief that the DAO should give away pizza, and the community embraced this belief with open arms. People said, 'Okay, I believe in that mission so I'm going to buy that NFT.' Together, the DAO and the community breathed life into the idea that pizza should be free.

"Using the proceeds from the launch, PizzaDAO gave away more than $300,000 worth of free pizza in 63 countries. The success of PizzaDAO's mission was a testament to the power of community and blockchain technology. Independent pizzerias now had access to the same resources as the big chains, and each member of the community had a stake in that success.

"In conclusion, PizzaDAO's mission to provide independent pizzerias with the same resources as big chains was embraced by the community. The use of blockchain technology and NFTs allowed for community ownership and investment in the DAO's mission. The launch was successful, and PizzaDAO's goal of giving away pizza was achieved. And so, the world of independent pizzerias was forever changed, thanks to PizzaDAO."

Melissa, the team's strategist, commented, "So cool. The PizzaDAO equalized the buying power and put it in the hands of the independent pizzeria owners. That's a very powerful strategy!"

Uniswap

Rex decided to head right into one of his favorite stories on DAOs: Uniswap.

"Uniswap is an interesting DAO example. Uniswap's governance is achieved through the UNI token, which gives holders the right to vote on important decisions and proposals for the platform. This decentralized governance structure allows for a more democratic and transparent decision-making process. Okay, I know that's a little boring. Let me tell it like a real-world fairy tale!"

The team quickly sat up for this funny way to share a case study.

Rex began with his dad voice. "Once upon a time in the world of Web3, there was a young programmer named Hayden Adams. He was frustrated with the centralized exchanges that dominated the market and their slow, outdated systems. So, he had an idea to create a decentralized exchange that would allow users to trade digital currencies directly with each other, without the need for intermediaries. He called this new exchange 'Uniswap.'

"Hayden built Uniswap using a new type of technology called an 'automated market maker' or AMM. This technology allowed Uniswap to create a market for any cryptocurrency, even if there was no trading activity for that token. This was a breakthrough and quickly attracted the attention of the community.

"As users started trading on Uniswap, they realized that it was much faster and more efficient than traditional centralized exchanges. The fees were lower, the user experience was better, and the platform was always available, no matter how many users were on it.

"Uniswap quickly became one of the most popular decentralized exchanges in the world. Its success was due to its innovative technology and its commitment to decentralization, which meant that users were in control of their own funds and had the freedom to trade with anyone, anywhere.

"As the popularity of Uniswap grew, so did its value. Investors began buying UNI, the platform's native token, which gave them a stake in the future of the exchange. The value of UNI skyrocketed, and Uniswap became one of the hottest projects in the crypto space.

"Today, Uniswap continues to thrive and innovate, cementing its position as a leader in the decentralized exchange space. The platform has become a symbol of the power of decentralization and the importance of giving users control over their own assets. It's a story that will be told for years to come and will inspire others to follow in its footsteps."

Decentraland

And Rex decided to share Decentraland as a DAO next.

"Many people don't know that Decentraland is a decentralized virtual world that operates as a DAO. It has an interesting design, governance, and use cases as a DAO. Decentraland is a blockchain-powered virtual world that allows users to create, experience, and monetize their content and applications. It operates as a DAO, meaning that it is governed by its users and decisions are made through a decentralized voting process.

"The Decentraland platform is built on the blockchain and uses smart contracts to enforce its rules and regulations. Users hold and control their assets through NFTs. Decentraland's virtual world is divided into parcels of land, which are also NFTs, and can be bought, sold, and developed by users.

"Decentraland is governed by its users through a decentralized voting process. Proposals for changes or improvements to the platform can be submitted by any user and then voted on by other users who hold Decentraland's native token, MANA. Proposals that receive enough votes are then implemented into the platform's smart contracts. This process ensures that the platform is continuously updated and improved based on its users' needs and preferences."

"So what can you do in Decentraland?" asked Greg.

"Well," responded Rex, "Decentraland has a wide range of use cases, including gaming, education, and social interaction. Users can create and play games, attend virtual events and conferences, and even build virtual real estate. Decentraland's virtual world is also home to several online marketplaces where users can buy, sell, and trade NFTs. This allows for a wide range of monetization opportunities, making Decentraland a unique platform for both content creators and consumers."

"Does the DAO make it more effective?" asked Melissa.

"Decentraland is an innovative platform that operates as a DAO, making it one of the few truly decentralized virtual worlds. Its design, governance, and use cases demonstrate the potential for blockchain technology to revolutionize the way we interact, create, and monetize digital content. Decentraland serves as a successful case study for the potential of DAOs to provide a more equitable and user-driven future for online communities. Its success will be told in future years."

L'Oréal NYX Professional Makeup

"And our final use case on DAOs is L'Oréal. I added this one in because it is an example of a brand using a DAO to garner the community around setting standards—in this case not a technical standard, but a standard of metaverse beauty," purred Rex.

"That's so essential when you really think about it," said Emma. "The value of beauty and inclusivity is yet to be defined there, and what better way than to engage an entire community. I really love that."

"So let me give you some details. The L'Oréal-owned brand NYX Professional Makeup is launching a DAO called GORJS to serve as an online beauty 'incubator.' You heard 'gorgeous,' but it is spelled G-O-R-J-S," punctuated Rex.

"The DAO aims to set a new standard for beauty in the metaverse and promote values of diversity, inclusivity, and accessibility. To support its goal, GORJS will also launch 1,000 NFTs called the 'FKWME Pass.'

"GORJS is a move beyond traditional physical cosmetics and aims to explore beauty in the digital age of avatars and pseudonymity. NYX Global Brand President Yann Joffredo believes that a new generation of Web3 creators will help redefine beauty and sees digital 'makeup' designs as offering unlimited possibilities beyond what's possible with physical cosmetics."

"Who can join this DAO?" asked V. "I really would like to be a part of defining beauty in the right way."

"GORJS members will use nontransferable governance tokens as voting chips for proposals and projects," Rex answered. "The community will make decisions through a more egalitarian power structure rather than a top-down one. Members can earn 'soulbound' GORJS tokens by purchasing a FKWME Pass NFT. The FKWME name was chosen because it represents the idea of joining and connecting with others who share the same vision."

As Rex completed his final use case on DAOs, he turned his attention to the use of AI.

Artificial Intelligence (AI) Tools

"AI has the ability to assist the rabbit team in a lot of projects," Rex began. "A survey by data analytics firm Teradata found that 80% of enterprise-level organizations were already using some form of AI in their business (32% of those in marketing). And the use of digital twins as AI-empowered industrial metaverses is already in use at more than 75% of industrial companies according to Altair's digital

"IN THE WEB3 AND METAVERSE WORLDS, AI HAS THE POTENTIAL TO BE THE ULTIMATE PARTNER—A TRUSTED ALLY THAT CAN HELP US UNLOCK NEW FRONTIERS, SOLVE COMPLEX PROBLEMS, AND BRING OUR WILDEST IDEAS TO LIFE. WITH THE POWER OF AI BY OUR SIDE, WE CAN EXPLORE UNCHARTED TERRITORIES AND BUILD A BRIGHTER FUTURE FOR ALL."

- Sandy Carter

twin summary report (https://altair.com/docs/default-source/pdfs/
altair_dt-global-survey-report_web.pdf?sfvrsn=b5aceaa9_28&_
ga=2.161266746.689901023.1682961156-1325679991.
1673542197&_gac=1.90975720.1680011913.CjwKCAjwoIqh
BhAGEiwArXT7K7qsxh-MLIpJPGbH4Z2GOX1sYtiNCcUeL
zvGk3izaOQNE3zWd_ebChoCotgQAvD_BwE__;!!N11eV2iwtf
s!pxWFAFZ6o6HuKip4ILx10on8K-molebEsT2MAXz_0JOjDp-
WWfcdWGGqQ45VFEXfPUojgTztqecU7uzEiyDH7g$).

"I'll share a few case studies of how companies are integrating, creating, and writing with AI tools today."

Unstoppable Domains

"Let's chat about how companies are using AI tools," continued Rex. "Unstoppable Domains is a digital identity company. It wanted to provide its customers new suggestions for a Web3 domain that acts as the customers' digital identity. AI tools made it easier to do customer engagement tasks by allowing users to find and claim their unique Web3 domain. Unstoppable Domains in fact used OpenAI's GPT-3—one of the largest models ever trained with 175 billion search parameters. Now, you can search for terms like 'company that sells coffee' and surface AI-powered ideas for your next domain. Leveraging the excitement around ChatGPT, it's a fun way to get ideas for your first (or next) Web3 domain that you fully own and control."

"Did they integrate this directly into their search?" asked Greg.

"Yes," answered Rex. "The new feature is integrated directly into the main search on UnstoppableDomains.com to inspire new domain ideas. The company piloted it first to get feedback and make improvements. Try it out. For example, type in 'Greg likes to cook keto recipes'—and search through your unique list of AI-generated domain suggestions, such as "ketocookingwithgreg.crypto," "greginthekitchen.crypto," or "ketogurugreg.crypto." It's that simple!

"This is a cool way to see the power of the ChatGPT APIs and the integration that is possible."

Gruppo Cimbalia

"Let's now switch over to a more industrial use of AI and the metaverse," Rex continued. "Digital twins are closely related to the concept of the industrial metaverse. An industrial metaverse is a virtual environment that allows for the simulation and optimization of physical systems and processes, such as factories or production lines. In this virtual environment, digital twins can be created to represent physical objects or processes and serve as their real-time digital counterparts. These digital twins can be used to monitor and analyze the performance of physical systems, predict and prevent failures, and optimize processes. Most of that analysis is done using AI.

"The example I'd like to share is Gruppo Cimbali, the leader in the production of professional espresso machines. They, along with their partner Altair Engineering, established a digital twin–driven development process for their coffee machines. This is a great example of how digital twins can be used within the industrial metaverse to optimize product performance and increase efficiency."

Rex paused to make sure this Rabbit team was still with him.

"By using digital twins to simulate and test Gruppo Cimbali's coffee machines virtually, they were able to reduce the need for physical testing and prototypes, leading to a 30% reduction in time-to-market, a 20% reduction in energy loss, and improved machine efficiency. This approach aligns with the goals of the industrial metaverse, which is to create a virtual environment where physical systems and processes can be monitored, analyzed, and optimized in real-time.

"Those are some very powerful results.

"The use of digital twins within the industrial metaverse allows manufacturers to simulate and test products and processes in a virtual environment, reducing the need for physical prototypes and tests. This approach can lead to cost savings, faster time-to-market, and more sustainable production practices."

Rex paused, since this example could be a bit more difficult to for the team to wrap their heads around, though it provided an impactful use of AI in the metaverse.

He continued, "Overall, the Altair and Gruppo Cimbali collaboration is an excellent example of how digital twins and the industrial metaverse can be used to revolutionize the way products are designed, manufactured, and maintained. After seeing the amazing advancements that digital twin technologies bring to the world of manufacturing while at several manufactures, this is the next phase for industrial technology—the use of AI simulation in the industrial metaverse."

NFT365 with Brian Fanzo

"And this next case study is just as fun," Rex started his next use case. "Brian Fanzos started a podcast called NFT365. He started out buying a new NFT each day (that's right, 365 days) and talking about it on the podcast. Now he has progressed to producing his own art using AI tools."

"What does he use, and was he already an artist?" asked Tommy.

"No, he isn't an artist. He tells of story of his daughters being ashamed of his art. He now uses Midjourney, an AI tool, and he uses prompts to set the mood, context, and scene in his mind. Just as we discussed earlier, the tool augments the intelligence, in this case, artistic ability!"

"Tell us a little bit about Midjourney," Greg urged.

"Midjourney is a generative AI tool that generates images from natural language descriptions, called 'prompts'", Rex explained. It offers a variety of customization options to help artists create unique and visually appealing NFTs. They also have an easy-to-use marketplace where artists can sell their NFTs to a global audience of buyers. By using Midjourney, NFT 365 provides 1 of 1 art now through the use of Midjourney. The art is unique based on the prompts from Brian, the artist. According to the current laws, this art then belongs to the artist. This may change over time.

"Let's move on now to NFT case studies on building engagement and community."

NFTs

"As a reminder," Rex began, "NFT collections are sets of unique, non-fungible tokens (NFTs) that are stored and managed as one. They usually contain groups of similar or related NFTs, such as digital art, collectible items, or in-game assets, and can be bought, sold, and traded like other NFTs. The ownership and realness of the NFTs within a collection are tracked and verified using blockchain technology."

Rex continued his use cases with one of his favorite NFTs.

Lazy Lions

"One of my friends is a queen in the Lazy Lions," bragged Rex.

"A queen? Like a real queen?" questioned V.

"Well kind of. She's a queen in the pride!" replied Rex. "Lazy Lions is a collection of 10,000 unique NFTs that are hosted on the Ethereum blockchain. The NFTs are algorithmically generated profile-picture-style avatars with more than 160 possible attributes that vary across each NFTs in the collection, ensuring their uniqueness. Members of their community are known as kings and queens."

"That's interesting, Rex," said Dawn. "Do they have a strong community element?"

"Yes, they do for sure," Rex replied. "The team believes that the project is the community, and the community is the project. They work with the community to deliver on their strategy rather than working in a silo.

"In addition, the community of Lazy Lions NFT holders have full commercial rights to their NFTs, access to an online community, and exclusive benefits such as ROARwards and access to a private island within the Sandbox metaverse. The creators drew inspiration from Assyrian culture and chose lions when designing their NFTs because of their cultural significance and representation of courage and strength.

"They've also been successful at forming tight brand partnerships with the NBA, Polygon, and Puma. Lazy Lions also introduced collectible trading cards to attract new members to the community. Owning a Lazy Lion NFT gives you access to a large and thriving community who shares the vision of dominating the future of entertainment and digital ownership through co-creation and innovation. Plus, all Lazy Lions NFT holders can earn ROARwards and participate in the project's Discord server for networking opportunities. I love this quote from Ashur, Founder of Lazy Lions: 'We envision a future where digital ownership and entertainment are intertwined, and Lazy Lions is dedicated to making that a reality.'"

"I'm going to have to go and check them out," Johnny broke in. "This whole new creator world is fascinating. Are there other NFT collections like this one?"

"Yes, there are," replied Rex.

CryptoPunks

"CryptoPunks is another success story of NFT engagement. In the world of NFTs, one project stands out as a trailblazer: CryptoPunks. Launched in 2017 by developers Matt Hall and John Watkinson, CryptoPunks is a collection of 10,000 unique 8×8 pixel art characters, each represented by a NFT.

"The project quickly gained popularity thanks to its unique approach to NFTs. With its limited number of characters, each with its own distinct traits and attributes, CryptoPunks offered a sense of scarcity and collectibility that resonated with users. The ability to buy, sell, and trade the characters on a secondary market only added to the appeal, creating a thriving trading ecosystem."

"Tell us about the community aspect," Dawn requested. "I'm forming a community strategy in my head."

"For sure," replied Rex. "CryptoPunks built a strong community of collectors, traders, and enthusiasts who were passionate about the project. This community helped drive engagement by sharing information, discussing strategies, and providing feedback to the creators. Additionally, the project's status as one of the first NFTs helped generate buzz and establish it as a pioneer in the NFT space.

"Finally, CryptoPunks' accessibility and ease of understanding made it appealing to a wide range of people, attracting a large user base and a loyal community of enthusiasts.

"Overall, CryptoPunks is a testament to the power of NFTs in engaging customers. Through a combination of scarcity, collectability, a secondary market, a vibrant community, pioneering status, and accessibility, CryptoPunks has cemented its place as one of the most successful NFT projects to date!"

V raised her hand and asked, "I've been reading about luxury brands too. Can you share about Tiffany's NFT adventure? It's one of my favorite brands."

Tiffany & Co.

"Of course. I'd love to share that case study," Rex said. "Luxury jewelry brand Tiffany & Co. made history by releasing a series of digital artworks as NFTs on the blockchain. The Tiffany NFT collection was a limited edition set of 10 unique artworks created by a group of talented artists and designers. The collection was sold through an online auction and generated significant interest and media coverage in the world of digital art and NFTs."

"Wow that's a big deal!" Melissa responded. "As an established brand, they have a lot on the line."

"Very true and they knew it," Rex agreed. "The luxury brand's reputation, the exclusivity of the NFTs, and the use of NFTs as a new medium for selling digital art helped attract attention and bidders to the auction. Social media platforms such as Instagram and Twitter were utilized to promote the collection and generate buzz, and the public was kept updated on the progress of the auction in real time. The artistic collaboration showcased the creativity and skill of the artists involved and added an extra layer of interest to the collection.

"And drumroll, please. The auction was a success, selling out within hours, with the highest bid reaching a staggering $130,000. The buyers of the NFTs were now the proud owners of a unique and provable digital asset, adding a new level of engagement for them as they own something exclusive and scarce. The collection also helped to build a community of art and NFT enthusiasts, who were able to connect and discuss the artworks and the auction."

"Weren't they one of the very first luxury brands?" asked Emma, loving the marketing angles on each of these stories.

"Yes. I would even say that the Tiffany NFT collection was a trailblazing example of how NFTs can be used by luxury brands to sell digital products and engage customers. The collection created a sense of exclusivity and rarity, showcased artistic talent, provided digital ownership, and built a community of enthusiasts. The story of the Tiffany NFT collection will forever be remembered as a successful experiment in the world of digital art and NFTs."

Blockchain Friends Forever (BFF)

Rex handed the mic over to V. Her best friend was one of the founding members of BFF, and V wanted to describe the specialness of the BFF NFT collection.

V began, "There is one other example I wanted you to hear about and that's one that's young and vibrant named BFF, short for Blockchain Friends Forever. BFF was created by Brit Morin and Jaime Schmidt, two serial entrepreneurs and investors who share a passion to help women rise to their full potential. Its vision is not just to revolutionize the art world by making it accessible to everyone but to help others understand the potential of this next phase of the internet. BFF began with 100+ founders who were passionate about the BFF mission of democratizing female and nonbinary education, access, and financial opportunity in the Web3 ecosystem."

"It's so exciting to see a group that is focused on both purpose and profit!" Melissa exclaimed. "I love the mission of helping get diverse viewpoints into this newly emerging space."

"I totally agree," said V. "BFF's membership model is in its NFT collections, which allow anyone, anywhere in the world, to own a piece of art and be a part of their digital community. The NFTs were created using blockchain technology, which ensured the authenticity and uniqueness of each piece of art.

"BFF's success was evident from the day it launched. The platform quickly gained a huge following, and its NFT collections were highly sought after. Collectors were drawn to BFF's unique approach to art and its mission to make Web3 accessible to everyone. The collections quickly became one of the most talked-about in the world."

"And how about the community aspect?" Emma asked. "This group must be super close."

"Yes, I would say so," V answered. "BFF's key differentiation was its focus on community. The team was dedicated to creating a space where art lovers and collectors plus those curious about Web3 could connect, share their passion, and learn from one another. Moreover, the team has provided education through events, newsletters, across social media and more.

"I would conclude this way," V added thoughtfully. "BFF's mission to revolutionize art and tech and make it accessible to everyone was a resounding success. Its unique approach to NFT collections and its focus on community set it apart from its competitors and made it one of the most valuable and well-respected brands in the world. BFF's story is a testament to the power of combining passion, technology, and community to create something truly special."

V passed the microphone back over to Rex.

"I hope you don't want my job, V. Nicely done," praised Rex. "But there is one more use case that's a different one for NFTs, but is so valuable."

Lowe's

Rex began his story: "Lowe's Companies, Inc. has created a Web3 proof of concept, Project Unlock, aimed at reducing organized retail crime, which costs retailers an average of $700k per $1B in sales. The solution involves the placement of RFID chips and internet of things (IoT) sensors in power tools that activate at purchase, creating a publicly accessible record of purchases to determine if the item was stolen or not.

"This is achieved by tying each product to a digital twin (NFT) on the blockchain, allowing resellers to check the status of the product to determine if it has been stolen. If successful, this solution has the potential to revolutionize the retail industry by turning every store item into an NFT, leading to trillions of NFTs around the world. The use of NFTs in this manner provides a secure and transparent method of tracking ownership, reducing the risk of organized retail crime, and protecting retailers from significant losses."

Conclusion

"Well, that closes out today's use cases," Rex said. "We did a lot in a day, and it's a lot to take in. Remember, I just shared 20 plus uses cases. There are hundreds out there. Make sure you continue to explore new examples. This is the new world. Examples of what's working can help shape your decisions a lot.

"I'm hoping as I went through these that you wrote down the value of the use case. For example, we saw strengthened communities, stronger engagement, and better experiences both for employees and customers. In addition, there were use cases that show how the metaverse strengthened internal collaboration in research and development as well as onboarding and hiring. And don't forget citizen engagement and government services effectiveness."

Rex paused. He really wanted the team to see the business outcomes.

"And the outcomes are yet to be written. Who would have thought that the PizzaDAO would have used a DAO for buying power or L'Oréal to define beauty in the metaverse. My favorite use case hasn't even been written yet!" he exclaimed.

V stood up. "Well, that concludes our weeklong education sessions. Now the hard work begins. We will begin with a week of Playstorming time, and then move into the strategizing and planning our bold vision!" V said. "It's going to be a tough time but fun. As my friends at AWS say, 'Let's make history!'"

With that, the team left for the weekend with their many notes and resources. They would be ready to make history and have fun!

5 | The Rabbit Team Plays

Let's Get Started!

Bright and early on Monday morning, V was ready for the day.

She wanted to start the "play" session off with a temporary coffee bar and scone setup outside the meeting area to get the creative juices flowing and set the tone for an enjoyable and productive session.

The coffee bar was set up to serve latte, cappuccino, Americano, nitro cold brew, and iced latte—all favorites in the Austin scene. Specialty coffee shops in Austin often offer unique and creative coffee drinks made with high-quality ingredients, so a wide variety of options were available, even with a barista to stir them up for the team.

The scones came from Frances's Scone Loft. Frances's made them with the finest ingredients and baked fresh on-site. V had selected several favorites, including blueberry, cinnamon sugar, lemon poppy seed, chocolate chip, and cranberry orange. In addition, for her rabbit team, she added in carrot cake too. She chuckled at her little joke!

The team was called the rabbit team as they were headed down the rabbit hole. This started with a few weeks of education—with the first week focused on more lectures and fireside chats on the technology. The second week focused on use cases and some real-world examples. Rex, the instructor, had warned that the pace was moving fast so they need to learn and be curious each day.

V sighed. She was ready for the day and thought the setup was the perfect way to start before the play session and even for later, when they'd be taking a break from the virtual world to relax and recharge.

As the team gathered around, V was so pleased with the talent she'd selected.

Dawn Alek was an excellent educator and had asked all the right questions on what methods and needs were required in this space. Tommy Seaport, her game lover, had been drawing ideas based on many of the elements in the games. With the convergence of virtual reality and real-world experiences, his skill sets were invaluable. Johnny Poyhonan was an expert in designing new products, having first started out in product management for Airbnb and TikTok. Neither was supposed to have become a big market mover, but both did.

Melissa Pop was the curious strategist who knew how to not just deal in theory but in real-world applications. She had helped lead the efforts for companies like 3M. Post-It Notes, for example, were originally intended as a repositionable adhesive for use in 3M's microfilm lab. But thinking outside the box on the possibilities, they became a useful tool for office and household organization. She'd gone on into tech, continuing to think big but executable.

Emma Sphynx was a marketer extraordinaire having built comm-unities for Reddit and Nike. With its large and active user base, Reddit is one of the best communities for brands to engage with potential customers and build their brand image.

And finally, Greg Dashed. His tech skills were legendary, and some called him the next Steve Wozniak!

Surveying the Surroundings

For the first day, the team was going to play with some technology that had been woven into the daily lives of most people.

V wanted the team to increase their curiosity. The CEOs of YouTube, PayPal, and Slack were all liberal arts majors. Given the rapid pace of innovation in the tech sector, skills like "learning how to learn" and approaching tough problems with a versatile skill set are often more valuable than deep expertise in any specific programming language, tech platform, or software package.

V kicked off the day with a few statements.

"Borders are merely illusion. The metaverse can sometimes be thought of as separate from what we do today, but in fact, some of the tech has already woven itself into the fabric of our daily lives. Thus, as you set forth on your journey into the metaverse, it is wise to first take heed of what surrounds you.

"Today we will play with a set of technologies like Alexa, live streaming, and more. Take note of the search engines that guide you, the virtual shop assistants that serve you, and the voice-activated devices that heed your every command."

V paused.

"Although they may not be full-fledged metaverses, these tools nonetheless hold the power to show you the way, introduce you to new companions, and help you navigate the digital world. These technologies serve as building blocks for the metaverse, which will likely be used in some form or fashion in the new immersive internet that combines elements from many of these existing technologies."

So the team spent time exploring tech like virtual assistants such as Alexa, VR and AR devices and software, along with social media platforms. In addition, they spent time on video conferencing and an array of collaboration tools and then turned to 3D modeling and animation software.

Being introduced to digital marketplaces and e-commerce platforms, they learned about consumer behavior and purchasing patterns as well as marketing strategies and user experiences.

Finally, at the end of the day they played with wearables and IoT devices. V had arranged for a jacket that sensed your mood and a ring that would call for help if touched. In addition, they played with smartwatches for health and fitness tracking, messaging, and phone calls. V introduced smart thermostats for the home and for industrial use, as well as security devices that were triggered from a smartphone or tablet.

Want to Play a Game?

V kicked off day 2 with a little chuckle.

"Yep. Tommy selected the agenda for today! You guys get to play video games all day long! Games are great examples of where the metaverse is headed."

So as Tommy headed to the front, he laid out the agenda for the day.

"READING ABOUT THE METAVERSE IS LIKE READING ABOUT A WILD ADVENTURE, BUT PLAYING IN IT IS LIKE ACTUALLY LIVING IT. THE METAVERSE IS A WORLD OF ENDLESS POSSIBILITIES WHERE WE CAN UNLEASH OUR CREATIVITY, CONNECT WITH OTHERS, AND EXPERIENCE THINGS WE NEVER THOUGHT POSSIBLE. SO DON'T JUST READ ABOUT IT— JUMP IN AND PLAY!"

– Sandy Carter

"We are going to immerse ourselves in gameplay," Tommy explained, in his element now. "The games I've chosen offer a glimpse into what a metaverse could look like and demonstrate the potential for virtual worlds to serve as shared spaces for social interaction, gaming, and creative expression.

"Some of these games are already in the Web3 space, like Roblox with its NFT launch. But we will play all day to get our hands dirty understanding what everyone is excited about."

V had been clear about wanting to ensure that the team got to play, and learn, not listen to lectures all day. The only exception was that Super Social was coming in to show off some Roblox examples toward the end of the day.

The team mainly focused on five games.

- **Second Life:** The very first virtual world where users create avatars and engage in a range of activities such as socializing, commerce, and creative expression.
- **VRChat:** A social VR platform where users can create and explore virtual environments, interact with others, and participate in various games and activities.
- **The Elder Scrolls Online:** A massively multiplayer online role-playing game (MMORPG) set in the world of Tamriel, where players can explore, quest, and engage in combat with others.
- **Fortnite:** A very popular and influential game that features a vast open-world environment where players can participate in battle royale–style combat, build structures, and engage with other players in real time. The social features, cross-platform play, and the constant introduction of new content have made Fortnite a hub for gaming, socializing, and entertainment.

- **World of Warcraft:** A popular game set in the fantasy world of Azeroth, where players can explore, quest, and engage in player-versus-player combat with others.

Tommy guided and assisted everyone all throughout the day until their guest showed up to walk them through Roblox.

The guest Roblox expert visited in person to maximize his time with the rabbit team. His name was Yon Raz-Fridman, the CEO of SuperSocial.

He began by explaining Roblox: "Roblox is a massively multiplayer online game platform that allows users to create their own games and play games created by other users. It's designed to be accessible to players of all ages, making it a good starting point for beginners who are new to gaming and online communities. The platform offers a wide variety of games, ranging from simple platformers to complex simulations and role-playing games. Players can interact with each other through in-game chat, creating a social aspect to the platform. Because it is so easy to use, Roblox has 250+ million monthly active users and 43.2 million daily active users, with 67% of users being under the age of 16."

"Under the age of 16?" Greg asked.

"Yes," Yon confirmed. "And the engagement on the Roblox platform is high, with daily active users spending an average of 156 minutes or 2.6 hours per day on the platform."

"How does it get that high engagement?" asked Dawn.

"Great question," responded Yon. "User-generated content is one of its secrets. Roblox allows users to create their own games, which adds to the platform's overall variety and keeps players engaged. And there's also a social aspect. Did you know that Roblox has a built-in social network, allowing players to play games with friends and meet new people? This creates a sense of community and keeps players coming back."

"There's that community word again," said Tommy. "Community is so very important in all of these virtual experiences."

"Right again," responded Yon. "And Roblox is designed to be accessible to players of all ages and technical abilities, which makes it appealing to a broad audience. The platform has a diverse user base, with 51% of users being male and 44% being female. And that accessibility extends to platforms too. Roblox is available on a variety of platforms, including desktop, mobile, and gaming consoles, which allows players to play with friends regardless of their preferred device.

"Oooo, and did I mention that you can make money on the platform too? Developers and creators on the platform have made more than $328 million, with 70% of game purchases going to the developers and 30% going to Roblox. Roblox's user base, engagement, and revenue continue to grow, making it a significant player in the online gaming industry."

"Are they already using Web3?" Greg inquired.

"They've started," Yon answered. "Roblox uses NFTs to represent unique virtual items in its platform, such as limited edition in-game items and avatar accessories. These NFTs are stored on a blockchain and can be bought, sold, and traded on the Roblox platform. Owners of these NFTs have verifiable proof of ownership and can prove the rarity and authenticity of their virtual items. This allows for a new level of scarcity, collectability, and ownership for virtual items on the

Roblox platform. I'm a big fan. We use it with many customers who are big brands."

"Really? Already?" asked Melissa. She was assessing how far behind EdgyMaven might be.

"Yes," responded Yon. "The experiences that we've build are not merely 'games'; they are worlds that illustrate our approach to living in the metaverse—worlds that power creativity, foster inclusivity, and drive prosperity. I'd describe it as 'the internet's home page' for a new generation. In fact, my company is setting out to build the Nintendo of the metaverse age with products that make a lasting impact on fans. And we do that with Roblox!"

"What's your secret sauce when working with brands and companies like ours?" V asked.

Yon laughed. "The secret sauce is combining creator talent who grew up on the Roblox platform with creatives and operators with decades of experience building consumer brands and telling stories in creative ways. My team combines deep Roblox expertise with AAA experience and creative storytellers who, together, design cutting-edge experiences that feels authentic to metaverse communities."

"I cannot wait to play!" V responded excitedly.

"The last thing I will add before you guys start trying it out is that Roblox is a well-run company. They keep it fresh. Roblox frequently releases updates and holds events, which keeps the platform fresh and engaging."

The team spent the rest of the day and some even into the night because they were having fun earning Robux, a premium currency within the world of Roblox that can be used to buy new games, private servers, and some other goodies.

"I just cannot believe how easy this is and fun!" squealed Melissa. The team had never seen her this excited. "I need more Robux to finish designing my business."

And that statement really summed up the day! V left many members of the team in the conference room as she hurried home to plan the next day.

Let's Go to a Virtual Conference and Concert!

On day 3, V had again set up a great day. Along with the usually treats, like the coffee bar, she added a lunchtime food truck visit from Discada.

Discada really had great TexMex food. And just as a note, Discada only serves one kind of taco— a "discada-style" taquito filled with a kitchen-sink combination of beef, pork, onion, and bell pepper slowly braised in a tractor plow disc that's been welded shut to resemble a shallow wok. This technique has been around for generations in Northern Mexico. Discada had modernized it a bit, gave it a Mexico City Street taco spin, and the result was an irresistibly flavorful, insanely consistent taquito that takes the cake for the best tacos in Austin.

The team would be so excited, not just for the tacos but because today they would be attending virtual events and even a virtual concert.

Attending virtual events in the metaverse provides a unique and valuable learning experience.

V kicked the day off with her logic on why the team attending virtual events made sense.

"In the metaverse," she began, "attendees can engage with others from around the world in a highly interactive and immersive environment. This will allow each of you to have another hands-on learning day and a set of networking opportunities too." She really emphasized networking.

"First, I'd like each of you to write down who you think you'll meet at these events in the metaverse. And then at the end of the day, I'd love each of you to come and tell me the types of people you met."

Everyone in the class began writing down their top three, and as V peeked to see what kind of answers she was getting, she saw that the answers ranged from kids to AI bots.

"Since the metaverse offers a lot of interactive features, which makes learning more fun and engaging," V continued, "I'd also like you to write down any good experiences that you think really grab your attention that you think that EdgyMaven should try too.

"Overall, attending a virtual event in the metaverse can be a great way to gain new skills and knowledge while also enjoying a unique and engaging experience."

They lined up for their assignments. The first thing they noticed was how many conferences and lectures were offered in the metaverse. There was also a session with Unstoppable Women of Web3 and the Metaverse in their headquarters in the Metaverse on Diversity in the space. Unstoppable Women of Web3 and the Metaverse had recently won an award for Best of Show at CES, and Emma, Melissa, V, Dawn, and Tommy (a father of daughters) were eager to try it out.

Then the best. They would all be attending a concert in the metaverse.

V excitedly shared, "Did you know that 10 million users attended Marshmello's Fortnite concert, which gave way to Fortnite's popularity in hosting metaverse performances. With the Marshmello avatar and a healthy dose of (virtual) pyro and raving, Marshmello's metaverse performance made history as the first concert in Fortnite. We will be experiencing a virtual concert tonight too."

V had gathered the list of virtual events in the metaverse by googling and using AI tools as well. She had come up with a list of more than 20 events for her team to experience. In addition, she had planned this day to occur on a night with a Roblox concert!

Some popular virtual concerts in the metaverse had included those hosted by platforms like Fortnite, Sandbox, and Decentraland. Those featured performances by well-known artists and were attended by thousands of people.

"The success of these virtual concerts is a testament to the growing popularity of virtual events in the metaverse, and they may set the standard for future virtual concerts to come. Let the virtual events begin," she said as she charged to a station setup in the conference room.

After the day of attending virtual events in the metaverse, V asked the team, "Tell me about the people that you met in the metaverse."

"I'll start," said Emma. "I was surprised. While in a Roblox event, I met a group of young girls designing their bedrooms. I also met CEOs and chief marketing officers at a virtual class hosted in the metaverse about future technology. At the Unstoppable Women of Web3 event, I even met leaders for Web3, blockchain, AI, and metaverse companies and got to ask them questions."

"And I went to a coding hackathon in the metaverse," said Gregg, "and met technologists from around the world. Singapore, Israel, England, Iceland, and more. It was incredible."

V asked, "Were you guys surprised at the level of people in the events?" As they nodded, she continued, "Gaming and the metaverse have moved out of the basement and into the boardroom."

And then they all left to change into their virtual outfits for the concert.

Being at the virtual concert in the metaverse was an immersive and interactive experience.

The concert took place in Roblox, where the team explored the environment and interacted with objects, other attendees, and even the performers themselves.

The concert featured live music, which in this case was experienced in real time.

Team members customized their avatars with AI tools.

They were able to dance, sing along, and Greg even played an instrument.

At the end of the concert, they were all exhausted. V ended the day with a simple insight: "That virtual concert in the metaverse gave us a glimpse into the future of a unique and interactive experience. This time for music fans. But imagine what is coming!"

Setting Up a Wallet and Funding It with Crypto

Day 4 started a little later as they had danced the virtual night away!

So, for this half-day session they were going to set up a wallet, buy crypto, brand their individual digital identities, and then explore several of the NFT marketplaces like Rarible, OpenSea, and MagicEden.

"Today will be a little bit tougher," V began the day. "We are going to set up a crypto wallet, put money in it, set up our digital identity. We will use Unstoppable Domains. Then set up our personal brand, and finish up by exploring NFT marketplaces."

She paused.

"Here's your list of instructions for the day. I'd like you guys to try to do this exercise on your own, without help in real life. There are many YouTube videos and other resources online. One of the complaints about Web3 is that it is still hard to set up a wallet. Experience the pain too. We heard of one NFT collection that failed because they didn't recognize the gap in ease of use." V stopped for effect. "I don't want that to be us."

"It won't happen on my watch," Dawn quickly commented. "However, that story was a great one to learn from. We've now spent weeks learning. Our customers won't take that time."

"You are right on it," replied V. "Now let's go and see what we can learn about these experiences compared to our gaming and virtual events in the metaverse!"

She left them with the following instructions: "First, I'd like you to read through Satoshi's white paper on Bitcoin. It will help you understand the basics. It's at https://bitcoin.org/bitcoin.pdf.

"Then you will select a wallet. There is no right or wrong answer. There are hundreds of wallets in the marketing, the space is constantly evolving, and the number of wallets changes quickly. Some of the ones you could consider are MyEtherWallet, Exodus, Metamask, Rainbow, and Trust Wallets."

Example Crypto Wallets:

- **MyEtherWallet (MEW):** A web-based wallet that is specifically designed for Ethereum and other ERC-20 tokens.
- **Exodus:** A desktop wallet that offers a user-friendly interface and supports a wide range of cryptocurrencies.
- **MetaMask:** A browser extension and mobile wallet that allows users to manage their cryptocurrency holding. It provides users with a secure and easy-to-use platform for accessing and managing their Ethereum-based assets, and it supports the storage of multiple cryptocurrencies.
- **Rainbow Wallet:** A noncustodial mobile wallet that supports multiple cryptocurrencies and is available for both iOS and Android devices.
- **Trust Wallet:** Allows users to securely store, manage, and trade their cryptocurrencies and digital assets, including Ethereum and all Ethereum-based tokens (such as ERC-20 and ERC-721). It is a noncustodial wallet.

V finished up the wallet section writing the ones she had mentioned on the board, knowing there were hundreds more. "Once you have chosen which wallet, you can create a new wallet by following the instructions provided by the wallet provider. This typically involves downloading the wallet software or visiting the website of a web-based wallet provider and setting up an account. When creating a wallet, you will be asked to provide personal information and set up a secure password."

Next, she warned them. "Your seed phrase is the only way to get access to your wallet or recover your assets if you forget your password.

It's very important to store it in a secure place. I'll emphasize this point: NEVER enter your private key/seed phrase on a computer, smartphone (such as in your phone's Notes app), or any other device. Don't take a picture of it, either. Also, NEVER share your private key/seed phrase with anyone. If any person or application asks for your private key or seed phrase, assume it is a scam. And ALWAYS store your private key/seed phrase in a secure place, out of sight. Write your keys down on at least two different pieces of paper and store them in separate places."

"You are scaring me, V," teased Johnny.

"Many people end up getting scammed in this way," V explained. "Next you will need to fund your wallet: Once you have set up your wallet, you can add funds to it by purchasing cryptocurrency from a cryptocurrency exchange or from a peer-to-peer market. To purchase cryptocurrency, you will need to provide the wallet address associated with your account as well as your payment information. Once the transaction is confirmed, the cryptocurrency will be deposited into your wallet, and you can use it to send and receive payments or hold it as an investment. Just do something small to experience it. EdgyMaven will fund you some ETH so that you can play with it, so come up to me once you have your wallet address."

"Everyone with me so far?" V asked.

"Yes, we are," answered Melissa and Dawn.

"Okay. Next up, go and check out some NFT collections on OpenSea, Rarible, and Magic Eden. Play around and have some fun!"

As the group broke, they grabbed a coffee and some snacks.

At the end of the day, the team regrouped.

"What did you think?" V asked.

Everyone except Greg and Tommy had a hard time.

"That's because Greg and Tommy have a depth of technical expertise and some crypto experience," V explained. "Some people may find the process of setting up a crypto wallet to be straightforward and easy, but most find it confusing and challenging. The process seems daunting."

"For me," admitted Emma, "it was securing my private keys and understanding the various features and options available. I felt overwhelmed by the various terms and concepts involved in using a wallet, such as public and private keys, seed phrases, and wallet addresses."

"I can see that," said Johnny. "I think only individuals with prior experience find the setup process to be relatively easy and straightforward."

V warned, "Many first-time users may feel nervous about setting up a wallet, as they are handling and storing their funds themselves. They worry about losing access to their funds due to technical issues or security breaches. That's why we may need to help them with extra steps so they can educate themselves and ensure the security of their wallet."

And with that Dawn smiled. She knew she had a big task in front of her.

Securing Your Digital Identity and Web3/Metaverse Branding

Finally, day 5 had arrived.

V believed in keeping her team healthy so she started the day with a nature walk around the park near the office. She had granola bars and takeout tea and coffee ready for the team.

Walking in nature has numerous benefits for both physical and mental health. It has been shown to reduce stress, improve mood, and improve focus and concentration. Plus both Emma and Tommy loved to hike and be in the outdoors. And while most of Johnny's activity had been in NYC, he had learned to love the smell of nature as well.

V strongly believed that spending time in nature had a calming effect on the mind and body, making it an ideal activity for those who need to break from the screens.

Additionally, it was a fun way to just chat about the weeks that they had been immersing themselves in Web3, the Metaverse and AI.

After their walk, they began their adventure of creating their digital identities and then branding themselves.

V had decided ahead of time to use Unstoppable Domains for their personal digital identities. Not only would it make it easier to do crypto payments, by using a human-readable name, Unstoppable Domains had differentiated itself by having the most integrations and the most utility of the digital identity.

Clearly her favorite, she explained, "You own, not rent, your digital identity from Unstoppable. I wouldn't want to rent or subscribe to something so precious. I do believe that owning my digital identity is a human right.

"Now let's get to it!"

They went to the site and found it easy to create their identities, choose their names, and get started.

After they had selected their Web3 domains, they began the thoughtful part of the day: defining their digital brands.

V said, "Our next exercise is very personal. Each of you will individually define your brand values and mission with the ethos of Web3 and the metaverse."

"You mean a personal brand?" asked their marketing expert, Emma. "I'd be happy to assist anyone as well. May I share my thoughts here, V?

"I was hoping you would," V answered.

"Creating a personal brand involves establishing a unique and memorable reputation for yourself in the minds of others," Emma explained. "The key elements of creating a personal brand include defining your values, skills, and strengths and then using that to create a consistent image across all your Web3, the metaverse and AI platforms. It will be important that you consistently demonstrate your expertise and deliver on your promises."

"A great example would be me as a change agent for EdgyMaven in these new technologies," V thoughtfully added. "For my brand I want it represented by a strong focus on education and certifications, as well as maybe NFTs that support education in others. Like Miss O'Cool girls who has an NFT collection dedicated to young girls."

"That's right," Emma agreed. "My marketing experience shows that a personal brand is more than just a logo or tagline; it is the culmination of your experiences, skills, and values that sets you apart and makes you stand out in your field. Building a strong personal brand requires effort and intentionality, but it pays off in terms of greater opportunities and recognition in your personal and professional life."

V then added to the personal branding section.

"To do this right, you will need to also understand your Web3, the metaverse and AI target audience. It could be a gaming crew or sustainability."

"Ah, I get it," said Dawn. "We are doing this for ourselves, and then we will do it for EdgyMaven."

"Am I that transparent," laughed V. "That's right. We will use some of these same steps for our corporate branding in Web3, the metaverse and AI.

"Next you will develop your consistent visual identity. You will have the opportunity to show that in your profile page on UD.ME/V. NFT or whatever your digital identity is!

"And finally, you will create your Web3, the metaverse and AI narrative to foster trust and transparency. And lastly, I want you to think through how to measure and then how often you will refine your brand strategy."

The team had fun with the exercise, all the while thinking about EdgyMaven too.

Some team members included sustainability badges or gaming levels. Some showed off their new wearables from DressX to indicate their sense of fashion.

After a great lunch, and another walk around the lake, the team settled into their next and last assignment.

Artificial Intelligence to Augment Your Skills

For the second half of the final day, the team was eager to start playing with the AI tooling.

V began the day with the following statement: "AI is a tool, but it's like having a partner on your project. And as far as partners go, they are dependable and hard-working but require guidance, direction, correction, and care. However, despite their shortcomings, having AI as a partner will let you do more, faster and better."

She listed out some of the tools, but she wanted them to explore as well. "I want you to spend several hours with chatbots and conversational AIs like Dall-e and ChatGPT. But in addition to these tools, check out CommonSim-1, which uses generative AI to produce 3D models and videos from a single image or description in text. And then Mem, which stands out with its AI-powered software that can parse through different notes, summarize them, and format them too. And I thought Midjourney would be fun to explore. We saw in the use cases that it can help with the development of actual NFT art. I don't know if that will be our approach, but let's experiment with it."

"Any tools for coders?" asked Greg.

"Well first, Greg, I have friends who use ChatGPT for coding too. For example, explaining code. Using ChatGPT, take some code you want to understand and ask ChatGPT to explain it. In addition, I hear it's pretty good at improving existing code. Ask ChatGPT to improve existing code by describing what you want to accomplish. It will give you instructions about how to do it, including the modified code. And even rewrite code in the correct style. This is great when refactoring code written by non-native Python developers who used a different naming convention. ChatGPT not only gives you the updated code, it also explains the reason for the changes," V rattled off. Clearly, she'd done her research.

"And I have a tool that I'd like you to check out too, specifically for coders. It's called CoPilot. It's described as an AI-powered programmer and is aimed at professional coders. Essentially it spits out lines of computer code, making the process faster."

Greg nodded excitedly as he was ready to go, but the rest of the team still had some questions.

"Any design-based AI-tools that I could review?" Emma and Dawn asked in unison. Both were interested in educational use cases as well as designing for customers.

"I would love you to play with Descript, which simplifies audio and video editing, which we may need for educating our internal teams as well as our customers," V replied.

"And I think there are just a few more this project could find interesting. ElevenLabs Prime Voice. I read that it can generate anyone's voice from text that's basically indistinguishable from reality. Wordtune provides dozens of rewrite options for words, sentences, and paragraphs to dramatically increase your writing quality. Poised is the last tool I have on my list. It analyzes and coaches your communication style so you can ace that keynote or speech to the board."

Emma spoke up. "I just had a friend share with me a new tool called Tome. With one prompt it creates narrative-driven presentations. It also includes visual assets along with beautiful design. Kind of like some of the metaverse stories that we saw. Can I try that one too?"

"Of course!" V responded. "Go online and find the newest and best tools to add to your list! Before we break off and go and play, I wanted to frame out some of the ways that AI can be that great tool and partner.

"Let's talk about the assignment. I am looking for you to discover the role of AI and the outcomes. For example, it could help us with our Web3 and metaverse strategy, serving as a tool for brainstorming and acting like a sounding board for our approach. Or it could help us with concepting. For example, test it out as a creative generator for an NFT collection or for thought starters, maybe in a metaverse story for our internal engineering team or external branding."

V paused to allow the team to soak in the assignment. To her, it was about experimenting with the tools to help accelerate their journey in these new spaces.

"We should also experiment with its value in fine-tuning copy and taglines for production. And finally, play with how we launch and scale our micro audiences, test new creative approaches, and event build AI-assisted community managers. Given we are a small but mighty rabbit team, it could save us time, reduce spend, and even help us cover community manager responsibilities 24/7. Take notes on not just the tool and the role of AI, but the outcome it helped you achieve."

The team then went away to play and soon starting sharing their initial findings.

Johnny said, "ChatGPT may be the greatest partner in product management I've ever seen. I played with having the tool help me with some offering ideas, and then it help me create 10 milestones that would have to be achieved to reach the goal. A RAD tool indeed!"

"Wow!" Emma concurred. "I just had Dall-e write a press release for our announcement of our Web3 and metaverse strategy!"

"And I designed an NFT with Midjourney," added Melissa. "It's very creative. I could see how this could help us with an EdgyMaven NFT collection if we go down that path."

"And I had a spooky experience with ElevenLabs Prime Voice," said Johnny. "The voice was just like mine! But fun to be sure."

V almost cheered. "This is a great start. Let's continue our play and write down your results on the role AI played and the outcome you could see us using on the project."

At the end of the final day they were convinced that they were ready to tackle the next month's challenges: building a bold plan for EdgyMaven!

6

Bold Vision and Planning Tools

Summary

V was happy with the last three weeks.

- The first week, Rex had been introduced as an outside expert to do an education session on the technology.
- The second week, Rex led them through case studies and fireside chats on the business outcomes from the technology with real case studies.
- The third week gave time for the team to get their hands into the experiences with five packed and immersive days.

V wrote out a description based on what she had learned over the previous weeks. She shared it with the team.

Speaking with authority, V began, "I've defined something I call the Rabbit mindset. I want each rabbit team member to take on this mindset. Here's how I describe it."

She showed this on the screen while she read the words out loud.

"A Rabbit mindset is a forward-looking perspective on the future of immersive experiences and the internet, characterized by a focus on personalization, engagement, and value to users. Futurists who embrace this mindset view virtual worlds as open, interoperable environments that they can shape and evolve using AI tooling to augment their intelligence.

"They consider digital identity to be a crucial aspect of the future and want to build a seamless and secure experience for users, the community. The Rabbit mindset involves thinking about the internet in a new way, with a 3D dimension and an appreciation for the potential of the creator platform. These futurists strive to become world builders, using their understanding of technology and their creative abilities to build personalized experiences that meet their needs and the needs of others." The Rabbit Mindset, with its focus on agility and adaptability, emphasizes the importance of being able to adapt quickly to changing circumstances and user needs, which is critical in a rapidly-evolving field like immersive experiences. In the context of immersive experiences and AI, this means embracing open, interoperable environments that can evolve and grow alongside the needs of users and creators.

Now she and the team would spend the time they needed building out the rest of the strategy with the five emPOWERments model for the Rabbit Mindset.

V had compiled this model from working with many companies in this space, and taking all the great learnings from brands, emerging tech companies, and metaverse/Web3/AI startups to come up with a first pass of how she wanted the team and her to come up with experiments, plans, and a bold vision.

""WEB3, METAVERSE, AND AI ARE THE ULTIMATE DISRUPTORS, AND THERE'S NO PLAYBOOK FOR WHAT'S COMING NEXT. WHILE I CAN SHARE LESSONS FOR THOSE WHO'VE GONE BEFORE US, YOU NEED TO STRAP IN AND BRING YOUR A-GAME BECAUSE IN THIS UNCHARTED TERRITORY, ONLY THE BOLDEST INNOVATORS WILL THRIVE. IT'S TIME TO BREAK THE RULES AND CREATE YOUR OWN DESTINY."

—Sandy Carter

emPOWERment 1: Building the Rabbit Team

The first emPOWERment had already been set into motion. She had built her rabbit team. The term *rabbit team* was derived from the Web3 saying of going down the rabbit hole. Cleverly, the rabbit team would venture in! This was the most important step as all the other "empowerments" wouldn't work without the right team.

She'd been very thoughtful in her choices in skills and experiences. V had formed a team of trailblazers and thought leaders in their chosen skill sets. She also had combined talent in an interesting way. She had a mix of those who grew up in the space of gaming, tech with creatives, and operators with decades of experience building brands, creating products, and telling stories in creative ways.

She would kick off the week with emPOWERment 2.

emPOWERment 2: Using Your Digital Identity to Brand in Web3 and the Metaverse

As the rabbit team filed in on Monday, their assignment was already written on the board.

"I wanted to thank all of you for your passion in our last weeks for learning about the space," V began the day. "Now is the time to apply those learnings, as we continue to learn daily.

"Today we will focus on thinking through our brand for EdgyMaven in Web3, the metaverse and AI world. Just as we did for us as individuals, I want us to think through the elements for EdgyMaven. Emma, I'd like you to take the lead but get the entire team's input and ideas. We will fill out this form but won't let us confine us."

"I'm up for the challenge," Emma stated. "And I'll be very inclusive."

The worksheet she would walk the team through looked like a thorough set of thought exercises that would prove to be very helpful in framing up their Web3, the metaverse and AI branding strategy.

Worksheet: Web3 and Metaverse Brand

1. What does your brand stand for today? Is it specific to the current mindset?
   - Write down the current perception of your brand and consider if it aligns with the rabbit mindset.
2. Define your brand values and mission with the ethos of Web3, the metaverse and AI mindset.
   - Clearly articulate the values that drive your brand and how they fit into Web3, the metaverse and AI vision.
   - Define your brand's mission in a way that resonates with the target audience.
3. Know Web3, the metaverse and AI target audience and who you need or want to target.
   - Identify who your ideal customer is in Web3, the metaverse and AI space.
   - Consider the demographic, needs, and interests of your target audience.
4. Define consistent visual identity elements.
   - Establish a visual style that is consistent across all touchpoints and accurately represents your brand.
   - This may include color palettes, logo, and imagery.
5. Create a strong Web3, the metaverse and AI narrative.
   - Develop a compelling story that connects your brand.
   - Ensure that this narrative is consistent across all marketing materials.

---

6. How will you foster trust and transparency?
- Establish clear policies and practices to ensure that your brand is transparent and trustworthy.
- This may include regular reporting on metrics, open communication channels, and a commitment to ethical business practices.

7. Metrics
- Determine the key performance indicators that you will use to measure the success of your brand strategy in Web3, the metaverse and AI space.

8. How often will you refine your brand strategy?
- Set a regular schedule for reviewing and updating your brand strategy to ensure that it remains relevant and effective.

For the second assignment of the day, the team would build out a pass of EdgyMaven's digital identity.

A Web3 digital identity provides a secure and decentralized way to store and manage personal information online. By having a Web3 digital identity, companies have complete control over their information and decide which data they want to share with others. This enhances privacy and security because information is protected from hacking and data breaches.

In addition to security benefits, a Web3 digital identity also offers new opportunities for businesses. It provides a secure way to verify the identity of users, enabling new business models and services. It also helps to reduce fraud and counterfeits, as digital identities can be verified in a decentralized way. Overall, a Web3 digital identity is an asset that will play a crucial role in the future of the internet and the digital world.

The team built a visual representation in the Digital Identity Profile page using Unstoppable Domains as a base.

emPOWERment 3: Building and Growing the Community with Customer Obsession

In the weeks that the team was working on its strategy, members analyzed the community that they wanted to build based on their target audience and how they wanted to approach it.

Customer obsession was their mantra. Building backward from the customer ensured that it was not about the technology, but their customers' needs and wants.

"I built another worksheet to help us think through the decisions," said V.

"We will need this and refine as we go," replied Melissa, who was deep into her strategy.

"Yes, because building a community for Web3, the metaverse and AI requires a proactive and intentional approach," said V. "As I thought about it from the use cases we saw and the experiences we had, we should start by identifying our target audience and defining the needed values and goals."

As they worked on that, Johnny said, "I think next, we need to create a compelling narrative that resonates with our target audience and clearly communicates the unique value proposition of Web3, the metaverse and AI. This will establish a foundation."

"This is going to take us a while," V responded, "as we actively engage with our users through various channels, such as social media, online forums, and in-person events. I want to foster open and transparent communication within the community and encourage active participation and contribution."

Additionally, the team continually assess and iterate on their approach to community building, incorporating feedback from their audience and adapting to the evolving needs of the Web3, the metaverse and AI ecosystem.

emPOWERment 4: Developing World-Class Experiences with the Metaverse

As the team assembled, V laid out the task before them. From all the learnings, they would have to tackle a few things over many weeks.

They had already hosted an immersive education session and played with different metaverses.

Now, they set out to determine their business goals.

"Team, we can start with a focus on an internal metaverse use case, or one for our customers," posed V. "And let's look at the business outcomes we need. Number one is greater customer engagement, but we could get that from better products using a metaverse internally."

"And maybe we would do both over time," said Melissa.

They then spent time brainstorming the options and potential application of the metaverse.

As they started to define a clear vision and goals, they also wanted to include responsible metaverse goals too so that they protected their users and their data.

"We have to prioritize privacy, security, safety, trust, and a responsible and sustainable metaverse strategy," argued Greg.

And that all agreed as they set out to select a metaverse platform and maybe a partner to help them execute, especially for the first time.

The platform that they wanted to select had to support the long-term success of their Web3, the metaverse and AI strategy.

Next up, Johnny led the discussions on developing user personas to better understand the needs and behaviors of target audience in the metaverse.

"My goal is to design a user experience that aligns with target audience needs and behavior so that we have an effective and enjoyable user experience, increased engagement, and loyalty," said their ace product manager.

"Cheers to that," sang Melissa and Emma in concert as they began to plan for content creation. Their goal was to create digital assets, environments, and experiences that aligned with vision and goals—and of course, memorable and impactful virtual environments and digital assets.

And finally, they worked on the handbook.

"I'd like to give ChatGPT a try at the handbook," said Tommy. He loved having ChatGPT take the first stab.

"I think you are right," agreed Greg, "since we are looking for principles and guidance for responsible use of the metaverse outlined and ensure responsible use of the metaverse."

And with that, they had begun their metaverse strategy.

emPOWERment 5: Augmenting Your Intelligence with AI

While the team had already begun considering the use of AI tools throughout their journey, they now started to see how they could optimize that usage.

They were a small but mighty team.

"When selecting AI tools for a team, it is important to consider the specific use cases and objectives of the project," spoke Greg as the technologist of the group. "Some key factors to consider include the scale and complexity of the project, the desired level of customization, and the budget and resource constraints."

"Also," said Melissa, half joking, "it may also be useful to consider the level of expertise and experience within the team."

The team was looking at AI tools for all parts of their project.

"AI tools bring a lot of benefits for content creators," asserted Emma. "Creative people who understand how to use AI will replace those who ignore the technology over time."

"Here are some tips that we should use for us," said Greg who had extensively played with many of the tools. "Start with a general prompt to test what the AI tool presents to you and then gradually make it more descriptive to refine the results."

"Yes, in fact for text generation, I suggest providing context on the target audience to adjust the tone of the text too," Emma added. "For example, if you don't want the copy to be too structured or conventional, add in something in a causal tone. The more details about the purpose for a website, or for a tweet, the better the tool will respond and guess help on context and style."

"So if we use AI, what does the law say about that today?" Tommy asked.

V responded. "So far, the content created by AI is treated as completely original. But we will have to keep checking to see if that remains the same. Most AI tools grant you the commercial rights to the content you produce with AI. But we should always check the terms and conditions when starting to use a new tool."

"I want to add one more comment," Greg responded with his technology savvy. "Once the appropriate AI tools have been selected, it is important to ensure that they are integrated effectively with the existing technology stack, and that the team has the necessary training and support to use them effectively. Ongoing monitoring and evaluation of the tools should also be a part of the process to ensure that they continue to meet the evolving needs of the project."

Now let's get to this checklist of great AI tools.

Putting It All Together for the Board

The team was now preparing for their board meeting.

The elements of their board package included an overall assessment, a strategy and execution plan starting with experimentation and trials, potential revenue streams, and potential risks and mitigations.

Their overall assessment included growth potential and the competitive landscape. For their execution plan, they shared both internal and external use cases as well as how they would experiment and build a community plan.

Next, they added in sections on technology and infrastructure as well as their initial thoughts for legal and regulatory considerations, including their intellectual capital.

And finally, they included a business model with both the investment costs and funding and potential revenue streams. The revenue streams that they found most interesting were around virtual goods and experiences, advertising, stronger customer engagement, subscriptions, user fees, licensing and royalties, and strategic partnerships. These revenue streams could be generated by a variety of business models, including transaction-based models, recurring revenue models, and data-driven models. The key was to find the revenue streams that aligned with the company's goals, target audience, and core competencies.

In addition, the rabbit team recommended that they do an education series for the whole company so that they wouldn't be sitting on the sidelines. They were part of the new rabbit mindset!

V concluded this day with some wise words.

"We will not be just Web3, the metaverse and AI consumers. We will be Web3, the metaverse and AI contributors. The metaverse doesn't exist for us. We are becoming a Web3, the metaverse and AI company, and we exist for the world. This is our new rabbit mindset.

"You can see how these five emPOWERments must work and weave together. For instance, you can use AI tools through all the steps, even to come up with interview questions for your candidates. Ensuring your brand mission works for your metaverse audience is also essential. Nothing can be done in a vacuum.

"There is no playbook here, only drafts and starts of some work because we are in such early stages of the technology. We will consistently refine and optimize and keep learning and growing. And we will experiment with ideas throughout."

And with that, the board approved phase 1 of the plan, the rabbit mindset.

PART II

The Application

7 | The Five EmPOWERments Model

An Overview of the Model

Companies today are intrigued by Web3, the metaverse and AI. In fact, we see companies bifurcating. They are dividing into those who are boldly in and those who are scared. We've seen bold moves in Web3, the metaverse and AI from companies like Starbucks, Nike, Prada, and IKEA.

You are either in or you're out—and forward-looking people will be drawn to the companies that can fully articulate their plans and vision for building in Web3, the metaverse and AI.

But before you begin to approach the space, there are five critical things that we saw from V and her team that can create a great plan for experimentation, matching to your brand and customers, and eventually driving a customer experience strategy.

159

The triangle is used here due to its significance in overall environmental structures. When building roofs, bridges, airplanes, or other structures, engineers need to make sure that the structure can bear weight. Simply put, they don't want the structure—whatever it is—to fall down when force is applied to it. The shape that can bear pressure and stress very well is the triangle. While you are working on emerging technology, there will be a lot of pressure to conform to the old ways of doing things. This new approach must be able to withstand the stress and pressure that will surely come upon the mission.

Dividing the triangle up into five pieces forms these emPOWERments (see Figure 7.1). This word was chosen due to its definition. Empowerment means the process of becoming stronger and more confident.

Figure 7.1   The 5 EmPOWERment Model

When working in a new space like Web3, the metaverse and AI, your thoughts and clarity of action will become stronger over time as you learn and are curious. The confidence will come while deep diving into the space.

At the base of the triangle is forming the rabbit team. This is your foundation. Selection of a team is important in a Web3, AI, and metaverse organization because these emerging fields require a diverse set of skills and expertise as well as the ability to adapt and learn quickly in a rapidly evolving landscape. V spent a lot of time selecting her team, educating that team, and building the culture of that team.

Next is the step of branding for Web3, the metaverse and AI. Your narrative and story will shape your strategy and direction. Digital identity is the technology that links together the people-side of the metaverse and the ownership of data from a Web3 viewpoint.

Community is the ethos of Web3. The community is the project, and the project is the community. It aligns with your customer obsession strategy. Rex spent a lot of time walking through use cases and examples. In addition, he commented that the space was so very new that this had to be done continuously.

Next up is your metaverse experience. This new internet is all about immersive experiences. V's team immersed themselves for a week in all the new experiences to create their own thoughts about what EdgyMaven needed.

And finally, they learned to use the AI tools as a partner. Not something to replace their creativity but that could grow and expand it. It made them more effective and efficient as a team. V commented a few times that they were a small but mighty team. Usually in new efforts like this with emerging technology, the teams are small and tools are essential.

These emPOWERments cannot be in isolation. These powers are interlocked and interconnected.

Understanding and Gaining Value from the Five emPOWERments

The power of the rabbit team

In today's world, companies form tiger teams. A tiger team is a group of people with diverse expertise who are assembled to work on a specific task or problem. The term "tiger team" is often used in the context of organizations that have a critical mission, such as a military unit or a large corporation, and the team is assembled to address a specific problem or challenge that requires the skills and knowledge of a diverse group of experts. Tiger teams are typically organized to work on a specific project or task for a limited period and are disbanded when the task is completed.

In Web3, the metaverse and AI, the power of rabbit teams is more fitting. These rabbit teams are those who want to go deep down the "rabbit hole." While they are like a tiger team in that they have diverse set of skills, here the prime mission is to not address a specific problem but to unlearn what they know and relearn the concepts of a new technology and a new ethos. Some will come from the new world—Web3, the metaverse and AI natives—but many will be Web3, the metaverse and AI immigrants.

The power of your branded digital identity in Web3 and ownership

In real estate, they say the three rules are location, location, location. You might not think this translates to the digital world, but it does. We're just talking about a different kind of real estate—the search bar.

Having an easy and clear name for people to type into whatever search bar has become the digital equivalent of prime real estate space. CarInsurance.com sold for a record $49.7 million, so clearly some valuable space is out there.

While domains in Web2 have been tied to standard domain names and social media handles, in Web3 there is a new decentralized and portable option to build your digital identity.

The first step to protecting your digital identity is to claim your domain. In the Web2 realm, this meant grabbing your website and all the associated social media handles. In Web3, the first step is to grab your business's name and the most popular Web3 domain extensions.

Next is to build a moat around your digital identity.

Depending on your business, you might want to consider building more of a moat around your digital identity. As your business gets larger, the moat you'll want to create around your digital identity will also get larger. The costs of losing part of your audience to a copycat or even worse, a scammer, grows along with your business, so it becomes even more important to protect your digital identity.

It will be essential to your branding strategy.

The power of creating community through customer obsession

At Amazon, customer obsession is a company-wide belief that every individual employee has responsibility for delivering the best possible service to customers. By working together as a team, they ensure that their business becomes even more efficient and productive.

The meaning of customer obsession is that all decisions and processes stem from the needs, desires, and delight of the customer. An easy way to start building towards Web3, the metaverse and AI strategy is to simply focus on community.

The magic of NFTs, for instance, isn't just the artwork; it's the fact that holders feel like stakeholders in a growing product. You need to provide a place for your community to congregate and maybe use some of Web3, the metaverse and AI tools to do that. It also helps brands keep an open line of communication between decision-makers and the community.

Web3 is a new form of customer obsession where you're not just talking at an audience. You are having a two-way conversation. Your community shapes you and you shape the community. There is shared value creation going on.

Web3, the metaverse and AI experiences can be more powerful when they foster a sense of community and social connection among users. This can involve the creation of social spaces, multiplayer games, and other opportunities for users to interact with each other.

The power of developing world–class experiences in the metaverse

The creation of powerful metaverse experiences involves a combination of several different factors, including strong design, engaging content, and effective use of technology.

For example, the design of an immersive environment. The design of the metaverse should be immersive and engaging, with richly detailed and believable environments that draw users in.

It also needs to offer engaging content: The content within the metaverse should be compelling and relevant to the intended audience. This can include interactive games, educational experiences, social spaces, and more.

The use of technology should be seamless and intuitive, allowing users to easily navigate and interact within the metaverse.

The power of artificial intelligence

Artificial intelligence is critical for the creation of a Web3 and metaverse strategy because it enables organizations to efficiently and effectively navigate the complex and constantly evolving digital landscape. With the rise of Web3 and the metaverse, the amount of data generated and processed will increase dramatically, and organizations will need the ability to analyze and make sense of this data in real time. Artificial intelligence provides the capability to automate complex tasks, extract insights from large amounts of data, and support decision-making processes. Additionally, AI can help organizations personalize and optimize their Web3 and metaverse strategies by providing real-time feedback and recommendations based on user behavior. By leveraging AI, organizations can ensure they are making the most of their Web3 and metaverse investments and staying ahead of the curve in an ever-evolving digital landscape. Furthermore, AI can enhance the overall user experience by providing personalized and seamless navigation through the metaverse. Overall, AI plays a crucial role in the creation and implementation of a successful Web3 and metaverse strategy.

In the next five sections, you will dive deeper into each of these five emPOWERments.

How to Build the Rabbit Team

People are the critical element in any successful change of any kind in an organization. And Web3, the metaverse and AI aren't just technology additions to your strategy but also changes in your business model, governance process, and execution best practices. Today there really isn't a playbook in place, which would be a set of guidelines to help you create your playbook for your company. The rabbit team is important because the team has to deep dive and learn and be curious. The Web3 ethos is "going down the rabbit hole." This team will do this on a daily basis. Something will change every day, with new case studies, new technology, failing technology, and more.

You saw how V carefully took time to select her team based on a set of skills and expertise needed to achieve the goals of staying fluid and nimble while creating an actual strategy and execution plan.

- **Identify key stakeholders and decision-makers.** It's important to involve the right people from the start to ensure buy-in and successful implementation. Avoid excluding those who may be affected by the new strategy, but don't involve too many people because it can slow down the decision-making process.
- **Assess the skills that you need.** Make sure you think through the cross-functional nature of the project. Having a diverse team with different skills and expertise can bring fresh perspectives and ideas to the table. When hiring the team, sometimes having a Web2 person on the team can help, due to **his or her** experience. You will also want someone who lives and eats the new technology. Avoid creating a homogeneous team because it may lead to a narrow-minded approach. Encourage team members to share their expertise and ideas. The recommendation for these new emerging areas is to consider the following:
  - An expert in learning and development both for employees and customers. This space is so new that both the internal team and the customers will need to be trained. From our experience, many companies are finding they have to do a lot of education, just like they did in the early days of the internet, to create a great onboarding experience.
  - A metaverse user or gamer. You need someone who is native to the space and really and truly loves it.
  - A great product manager who thinks creatively and doesn't have to have a focus group to reveal the answer. Also search

for someone who is not constrained to the total addressable market (TAM). By the time there is a TAM, it might be too late anyway. Most successful products didn't really have a TAM. They built the TAM.

- A broad strategist. You will need someone to help you shape a strategy that moves and flows based on your experiments, mistakes, and successes.
- A marketer with community-building experience. The team needs someone who has created a community and believes in its power to make the company better.
- An amazing technologist. Select someone who plays with the new technology like the blockchain and AI but who understands the legacy technology and the ability to scale.

   Make sure you assess the skills and expertise of your existing internal team members and identify any gaps that need to be filled. But at the same time, identify external experts and consultants with relevant experience and expertise in Web3, the metaverse and AI space.

In addition, decide on the structure and formation of your team. Your structure depends on your company's culture. From the Vayner Web3 report, the demand for cross-functional teams in Web3-focused firms is increasing, as nontechnical positions such as marketing, management, and HR become more important in commercializing Web3 solutions at scale. This trend is reflected in the growth of nontechnical job postings, doubling from 2021–2023 and the hiring of dedicated Web3 teams by F500 companies across industries. These teams will play a significant role in internal education, evangelism, and community-building to drive broad Web3 adoption.

Large enterprises building dedicated Web3 competencies have adopted various operating models, including steering committees, centers of Enablement, and design studios. Each model has its pros, cons, and go-to-market motions, and they are expected to grow and evolve as enterprises develop more thoughtful processes and infrastructure around Web3 products and services.

Web3 Steering Committee. A Web3 steering committee can be a starting point for brands looking to explore the technology, providing cross-functional education and championship while minimizing disruption to matrixed organizations. However, it requires a high degree of cross-functional decision-making and alignment, which can be challenging. Additionally, it may not be the most efficient use of resources, as 10% of 10 people does not equal one full-time equivalent.

In summary, the pros of a Web3 steering committee include providing a starting point for exploration, cross-functional education, and minimizing disruption. However, it also requires alignment and decision-making across functions, which can be challenging, and may not be the most efficient use of resources.

Web3 Center of Enablement. A Web3 enablement team can provide a dedicated, tight-knit group to develop best practices, guiding principles, and initial concepts for cross-enterprise execution. This approach can be a "Goldilocks" approach for committed testing, with dedicated stakeholders driving accountability. It also offers flexibility for multi-brand execution. However, it still involves a meaningful commitment of resources.

In summary, the pros of a Web3 enablement team include a dedicated and tight-knit group for development, committed testing with accountability, and flexibility for multi-brand execution. However, it still requires a meaningful commitment of resources.

Web3 Design Studio. A Web3 design studio is a dedicated, cross-functional team that handles all strategy, design, and go-to-market

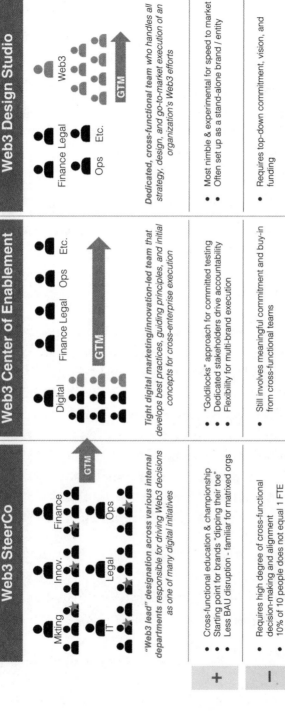

Source: **VAYNER3 - Web3 trends for 2023**

Figure 7.2 Types of Web3 Teams

execution. It is the most nimble and experimental for speed to market and is often set up as a stand-alone brand or entity. However, it requires top-down commitment, vision, and funding to be successful.

In summary, the pros of a Web3 design studio include being the most nimble and experimental for speed to market and often being set up as a stand-alone brand or entity. However, it requires top-down commitment, vision, and funding to be successful.

Worksheet: Forming a Rabbit Team

Here is a sample worksheet for selecting a team for a Web3 and metaverse project:

1. **The Educator**
   - Skills required
     - Strong understanding of Web3, the metaverse and AI technologies or ability to learn
     - Ability to educate and train others
     - Excellent communication and interpersonal skills
   - Questions to ask during the selection process
     - How would you explain the basics of a topic to someone with no prior knowledge?
     - How do you approach teaching complex concepts to others?
     - Have you conducted training sessions or workshops before?
     - Can you provide examples of successful training initiatives you have led?
2. **The Gamer/Lives in Metaverse**
   - Skills required
     - Passion for gaming and metaverse
     - In-depth knowledge of gaming trends and metaverse landscapes
     - Strong analytical skills to evaluate metaverse projects

- Questions to ask during the selection process
  - How do you stay up-to-date with gaming and metaverse developments?
  - Can you tell us about your favorite gaming experience in the metaverse?
  - Have you evaluated any metaverse projects before?
  - Can you provide examples of metaverse projects that you find exciting and innovative?
3. The Product Manager 3.0
  - Skills required
    - Experience in product management
    - Understanding of Web3, the metaverse and AI technologies
    - Excellent problem-solving skills
  - Questions to ask during the selection process
    - Can you tell us about your experience in product management?
    - How do you approach product development in the Web3, the metaverse and AI space?
    - Can you provide examples of successful products you have managed?
    - How do you prioritize features and balance trade-offs in product development?
4. The Strategist
  - Skills required
    - Strategic thinking and planning
    - Ability to identify and evaluate opportunities
    - Strong communication and collaboration skills
  - Questions to ask during the selection process
    - Can you tell us about a strategic initiative you led and the impact it had?
    - How do you approach opportunity identification and evaluation?

- Can you provide examples of successful opportunities you identified and evaluated in the past?
- How do you ensure effective communication and collaboration across teams?

5. The Marketer
  - Skills required
    - Understanding of market trends and consumer behavior
    - Strong marketing and promotional skills
    - Ability to analyze and evaluate market data
  - Questions to ask during the selection process
    - Can you tell us about your experience in marketing and promotion?
    - How do you approach market research and analysis?
    - Can you provide examples of successful marketing campaigns you have led?
    - How do you measure the success of marketing initiatives?

6. The Technologist
  - Skills required
    - Strong technical skills
    - Ability to evaluate and implement Web3, the metaverse and AI technologies
    - Excellent problem-solving skills
  - Questions to ask during the selection process
    - Can you tell us about your technical expertise and experience?
    - Have you worked on Web3, the metaverse and AI projects before?
    - Can you provide examples of successful projects you have worked on?
    - How do you approach problems?

- **Choose your overall structure:** Web3 steering committee, Web3 center of enablement, or Web3 design studio.
- **Define the roles and responsibilities.** Clarity on who is responsible for what will ensure accountability. Usually, a book would advise you to avoid vague or overlapping responsibilities because it leads to confusion and inefficiency; however, in this new emerging space, overlapping responsibilities can help open new innovative ideas.
- **Encourage open communication and collaboration.** The team is trying to make history, and members will need an open and transparent culture to foster innovation and creativity. Encourage team members to actively listen to each other and share their thoughts and ideas.
- **Set goals:** Having clear, quantifiable goals will give the team a clear direction and help measure success. However, this is a new space; sometimes you will have vague or overly ambitious goals. Ensure the team knows you will adjust as you go to avoid disappointment and frustration. You won't know what goals are realistic and achievable until you have some learning under your belt.
- **Set learn and be curious as a mission.** Staying up-to-date on the latest technology trends will help inform and guide the new strategy. Avoid relying solely on outdated information or disregarding potential game changers. Regularly assess the potential impact of emerging technology on the business.
- **Regularly evaluate and adjust the strategy and execution.** Regularly reviewing and refining the strategy will help ensure it remains relevant and effective. Avoid blindly sticking to the initial plan, especially if it's not working. Be willing to pivot and make changes as needed.

How to Build Your Web3 Digital Identity as a Company or Individual Brand

Your Web3 digital identity will be a digital asset, fully owned by you, that will holds all your data about yourself or your company brand. The moment you take your first steps into your Web3 and metaverse journey is the right time to start developing your Web3 and metaverse brand identity.

How do you get started building your Web3 and metaverse digital identity?

For both your personal brand and your corporate brand

- **Define your brand values and mission with the ethos of Web3 and the metaverse.** Always find a parallel between your Web3 identity and your brand in Web2. For instance, Tiffany's leveraged their Web2 strength in luxury branding to create a strong Web3 set of values and mission that were consistent with their brand story. An individual brand example would be to associate yourself with your value as an innovator and having all your brand elements support that. For Sandy.NFT, showcasing an innovator award would support that brand value.
- **Know Web3, the metaverse and AI target audience.** This audience will most likely be more crypto savvy and gaming enthusiasts with interest in immersive experiences. You will find a lot of creatives and artists in these areas too. Look for strong social media users and virtual event attendees. Early adopters and risk takers frequent this area as well as entrepreneurs and investors.

    The metaverse and Web3 technology have the potential to attract individuals from a wide range of generations; however, most early adopters and the most active users tend to be from the younger generations, including:

- Generation Z (born 1997–2012): This tech-savvy generation has grown up with the internet and digital technology, making them natural early adopters of metaverse and Web3 technology.
- Millennials (born 1981–1996): Many millennials are familiar with virtual environments and online communities, making them open to exploring the social and creative potential of the metaverse.
- Generation X (born 1965–1980): This generation is likely to be more familiar with traditional technology and may be more cautious about embracing new technology, but some individuals may be drawn to the potential for new business and investment opportunities in the metaverse.

  Web3, the metaverse and AI are still in their early stages of development, and it remains to be seen how widely adopted they will become across different generations.

  The most powerful element will be thinking who you need to attract in this space. The early adopters are driven by a certain mindset, but you will want and need to attract your audience. Think about how you could leverage these early adopters to influence your desired audience as well.

- **Develop a consistent visual identity:** The same advice for Web2 eases its way into Web3 too. Create a distinctive look and feel for your brand, including a logo, color palette, typography, and imagery, and use it consistently across all channels. That distinctive look and feel could come from an NFT collection or inspired metaverse or game world.
- **Create a strong Web3, the metaverse and AI narrative:** Tell a compelling story about your brand, highlighting its unique value proposition and how it fits into the wider Web3 and metaverse ecosystem. This could be highlighting partnerships with Web3, the metaverse and AI known players as well. Collaborating with known players provides credibility and trust and can give you permission to tap into other audiences.

- **Foster trust and transparency:** Especially with the Web3 ethos, be open and transparent about your policies and goals, and prioritize security and privacy in your offerings to build trust with your customers.
- **Measure and refine your brand strategy:** This phase will be used a lot as we are very early into Web3, the metaverse and AI era. Continuously monitor and analyze your branding efforts to understand what's working and what's not, and make changes as needed to optimize your results. Make sure your profile is up-to-date, professional, and reflects your brand.

Worksheet: Web3, the metaverse and AI Brand

1. What does your brand stand for today? Is it specific to the current mindset?
   - Write down the current perception of your brand and consider if it aligns with Web3, the metaverse and AI mindset.
2. Define your brand values and mission with the ethos of the ethos of the rabbit mindset.
   - Clearly articulate the values that drive your brand and how they fit into Web3, the metaverse and AI vision.
   - Define your brand's mission in a way that resonates with the target audience.
3. Know Web3, the metaverse and AI target audience and who you need or want to target.
   - Identify who your ideal customer is in Web3, the metaverse and AI space.
   - Consider the demographic, needs, and interests of your target audience.
4. Define consistent visual identity elements.
   - Establish a visual style that is consistent across all touchpoints and accurately represents your brand, including color palettes, logo, and imagery.

5. Create a strong narrative.
   - Develop a compelling story that connects your brand to the Web3, the metaverse and AI vision.
   - Ensure that this narrative is consistent across all marketing materials.
6. How will you foster trust and transparency?
   - Establish clear policies and practices to ensure that your brand is transparent and trustworthy.
   - This may include regular reporting on metrics, open communication channels, and a commitment to ethical business practices.
7. Metrics
   - Determine the key performance indicators that you will use to measure the success of your brand strategy in the Web3 and metaverse space.
8. How often will you refine your brand strategy?
   - Set a regular schedule for reviewing and updating your brand strategy to ensure that it remains relevant and effective.

For an individual Web3/metaverse digital identity

Note: In this example, the Unstoppable Domains digital identity profile page is used to illustrate a Web3 profile page. You can use the profile page to showcase all your digital information, very similar to a Web2 LinkedIn page that can show your brand to the world.

Your digital identity is made of data from your arsenal. These can be collected art NFTs, event tickets, awards, classes, digital assets, wearables, DAO voting, digital land ownership, and more. Once you decide on your brand and your visual identity, ensure you select those elements that support that brand image. Remember, since you own your data, you can decide what you would like to show.

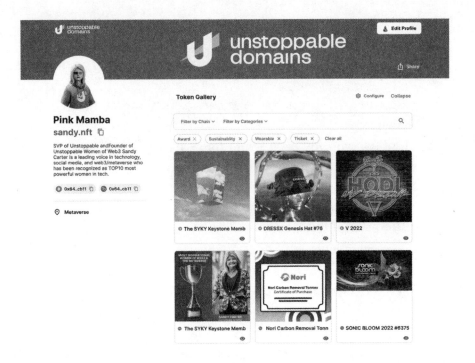

Figure 7.3   Digital Identity, Individual

An example is with Sandy Carter whose digital identity is Sandy. NFT. Start by going to UD.Me/Sandy.NFT. (If you are trying this for your own digital identity, go to UD.me/DI where your digital identity replaces the DI. Typically, that DI would be Nora.Crypto, or Lisa.X, or Seaport.NFT.)

On this page, you can review what data is stored in your digital identity today.

First, you can see the banner across the top. Sandy.NFT has chosen to use her company's logo since this is her professional Web3 brand. You can choose whatever fits your visual identity.

Next, you will see a picture next to the digital identity Sandy.NFT. This picture shown here is an Avatar, in this case from ReadyPlayerMe that can be used in over 7,000 metaverses. Chosen instead could be AI generated art, or a real picture of you representing your brand. Note that most Web3 and metaverse profiles feature an NFT or avatar as opposed to a real picture. This is one difference between Web2 and Web3.

Underneath is a short bio and your location. For Sandy.NFT, she has chosen the metaverse as her location. In this section, you could use New York or Singapore or any other location.

Under the bio and location, you see a link to your Web3 wallet. This enables Sandy.NFT to be used in transactions as well. In this example, you see Sandy.NFT has two wallets connected.

On the right-hand side, you will notice that what is shown next are a set of tokens (digital assets) stored in the Token Gallery. Here you can filter by a set of categories to support your personal branding, paying attention to the visual look as well as the message it is sending. For example, in Sandy.NFT profile page, you see a badge from Nori, a company supporting sustainability. This showcases a badge that Sandy.NFT has earned by neutralizing the carbon from an NFT.

Other tokens that could show your personal brand could be events you've attended or wearables you own. It could be a gaming level that you've achieved or educational certifications that you've completed. Even awards could be showcased in this section.

Just as you take time to create your LinkedIn page, spend time crafting your Web3 and metaverse identity.

Under the Token Gallery is your set of social media from the Web2 world. This could symbolize your bridging the Web2 to Web3 worlds and helps you earn status or reputation in Web3 social media applications.

Right beneath the social media section, is your Web3 decentralized website. For Sandy.NFT, that website is Sandy.NFT. Note that this decentralized website requires a Web3 browser like Opera, Brave, or Chrome with an extension.

Under the website are your badges. Since badges are issued based on a wallet's transactions, they're an easy way to build your reputation just by supporting whatever projects interest you. Badges allow you to represent your communities, affinities, and interests across Web3. New badges will be added so you can showcase your journey with crypto, NFTs, DAOs, and the rest of the Web3 universe.

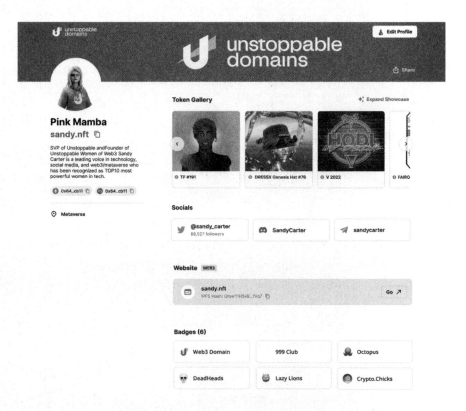

Figure 7.4   Digital identity, profile

For a corporate Web3/metaverse digital identity

Note: In this example, the Unstoppable Domains digital identity profile page is used to illustrate a Web3 profile page. You can use the profile page to showcase all your digital information, very similar to a Web2 LinkedIn page that can show your brand to the world.

Your digital identity is made of data from your corporate arsenal.

These can be sponsored NFTs, event sponsorships, your Web3 and metaverse offerings, and more. Once you decide on your brand and your visual identity, ensure you select those elements that support that brand image. Remember, since you own your data, you can decide what you would like to show.

An example is with a Partner Company whose digital identity is Partner.x. Start by going to UD.Me/Partner.x. (If you are trying this for your own company's digital identity, go to UD.me/DI where your digital identity replaces the DI. Typically, that DI would be Company. NFT or Company.blockchain.)

First, you can see the banner across the top. UD Partner has chosen to use its company's logo to show consistency across its Web2 and Web3 brands.

Next, you will see a picture next to the digital identity UnstoppablePartner.x. This picture shown here is a NFT collection that the UD Partner company has released.

Underneath is a short bio about the company and the company's location. For UnstoppablePartner.x, they have chosen the metaverse as they released a headquarters in the metaverse. Any location in the real world or in the metaverse could be used in this profile.

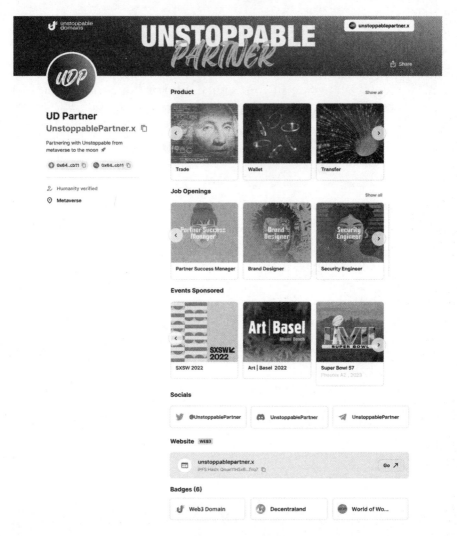

Figure 7.5   Digital Identity, Corporate

Under the bio and location, you see a link to the wallet. This enables the wallet to be used in transactions as well.

On the right-hand side, the company's products that exist in Web3 and the metaverse are showcased. For UnstoppablePartner.x, they have turned their products into NFT art and shown those consistent with its brand visual identity.

Under the products, UnstoppablePartner.x has showcased its Web3 and metaverse job openings. And following that are the Web3 and metaverse events that they have sponsored.

Other tokens that could show your corporate brand could be sustainability efforts your company is part of, or education on Web3 and the metaverse you offer. Even awards could be showcased in this section.

Underneath is your company's set of social media from the Web2 world. This could symbolize your bridging the Web2 to Web3 worlds and helps your company earn reputation or status in Web3 social media applications.

And finally we see a spot for your company's decentralized website.

Digital identity is a powerful concept and is the entry point for Web3 and the metaverse. As the internet becomes more immersive, people want to bring more of their "real selves" online; they want to create community and find their tribe. Start yours today!

Grow Community with Customer Obsession

Community is a special part of the Web3, the metaverse and AI ethos. And as you saw from the use cases, it is a big part of driving engagement, awareness, and brand loyalty. Web3, the metaverse and AI are the future of the internet and offer a unique opportunity for brands to build communities like never before.

By leveraging the new technology, brands can create communities with engaged, loyal, and profitable members who are invested in the community's success. How do you achieve this? Well, the rule book has not been written yet, but from early success we see that opt-in memberships, sometimes token gated, that offer exclusive access to buy-in and rewards, can lead to improved brand loyalty.

To build strong relationships with influencers, it's crucial for brands to be present in their communities and engage with like-minded individuals. And of course, you must be authentic.

Membership can serve as a tool for scaling and revenue generation, with members holding ownership and different types of memberships within a single community.

When building a community, it is crucial to move members up in levels of engagement instead of focusing on making everyone look like hyper-engaged champions. Therefore, it is important to have a broad and diverse community to attract and activate different kinds of folks.

To build a successful community, collaboratively create and track cohorts of members based on shared attributes. For example, everyone who buys certain digital assets or who writes posts about certain digital identity topics. This can be done by tracking community user journeys, segmenting users by their impact points, and progress as they become more active in the community.

It is also essential to identify product champion candidates by adding members to a segment with a certain number of posts, responses, or content created, and updating their status based on their eligibility for something that identities them as champions. For example, in an NFT collection, someone may consistently discuss the attributes of a collection. By following these critical elements, it is possible to create a community that attracts and engages a broad and diverse range of members, resulting in better feedback and product development.

However, building a Web3 community from scratch requires careful consideration and effort. Brands must be prepared to invest time and resources to establish themselves as an authority in their field or niche market and create an ecosystem that brings together partners, affiliates, and other stakeholders

A top saying is, "The community is the project, and the project is the community." And that's really the secret sauce in becoming a top company in Web3, the metaverse and AI. Everything your company does should be aimed at providing value to the community.

Good guidelines for building a community in Web3, the metaverse and AI are the following tips.

- **Choose the best platform.** From the case studies, different companies have used different tools, and you want to choose the platform that best fits your needs. From participation in a metaverse, to building their own metaverse to simply using available community tools—the options are almost limitless. The most popular tools are Twitter, Discord, and Telegram. You don't have to pick any of them. For instance, Twitter gives you access to key influencers and the ability to do Twitter Spaces to speak directly to the audience. Most NFT collections have Discord with dedicated channels to specific topics. Selection of your tool or tools should be dependent on your goals and mission.
- **Understand the Web3, the metaverse and AI ethos.** If your company wants to be a part of this new digital frontier, then you need to understand the unique and ever-evolving culture. It is very different than the traditional brand or Web2 culture that exists today. It is more decentralized in thought and approach. Start by learning the language. For instance, say gm, instead of good morning. It may seem minor, but it is important. Also get to know the different communities and what makes them tick. Hang out in Discord. Jump on a few Telegram groups. Join some of the metaverse classes. Once you learn, don't be afraid to add a touch of personality and creativity.

Some of the lessons learned from the use cases are around traditional Web2 companies starting to enter the Web3 world. This is awesome, and it is definitely encouraged, but there have been some missteps that could have been avoided. For example, because of the economics involved with NFTs, it can sometimes come across as a cash grab, which will alienate the Web3 world. Conversely, if not introduced well to the existing community, you run the risk of alienating them.

What's worked really well in the space is when traditional Web2 brands collaborate with established Web3 and metaverse brands to enter the space. Some great examples include Adidas with the Bored Ape Yacht Club. They released an NFT collection and generated $22 million within hours. Besides the economics involved, the true value that NFTs can bring brands is in deeper engagement with their community. It goes back to a simple principle that people care about the things they own.

- **Define a clear mission and purpose for the community.** Develop a strategy for your brand's Web3, the metaverse and AI community, including goals, tactics, and metrics for success. Of course, some of these will depend on the tools you choose. For example, a goal may be to share information once a week, and the tactic could be a special channel announcement on Discord or a weekly Twitter space!

- **Foster meaningful relationships and encourage collaboration.** Web3 is a group of builders or, as they like to say, "buidlers." The metaverse is a group of creatives and gamers. Make sure you encourage collaboration through places where the group can share their thoughts. For example, for Unstoppable Women of Web3, in their headquarters in Decentraland designed by H&N, they do weekly town hall meetings to garner feedback and do a weekly Twitter space.

- **Make it easy for members to contribute.** Easy is the best way. The Web3 mantra is to "give power back to the people," so let them know what they say, do, and suggest matters. It provides more meaning to your project. When brands gives value to their members, they are rewarded with loyalty.

- **Provide resources, support, and incentives to encourage participation and engagement.** Make sure you are sharing your support and resources with the community. For example, education on a subject or access to certain OGs (original gangster) in the space. Incentives and rewards are important too. For example, owning a Lazy Lion also comes with a bunch of perks out of the gate. One of the interesting perks being that you get the commercial rights to that individual Lazy Lion This introduces so much possibility into what can be achieved in an NFT collection together with the community.

- **Encourage diversity and inclusiveness.** Ensure that your community is diverse in its thoughts and actions. Figure out ways to encouraging representation from diverse backgrounds in leadership and decision-making roles within the community. Many communities have now implemented inclusive design principles in the creation of virtual spaces, avatars, and events.

  And ensure that you are regularly gathering feedback and input from community members and using this information to continuously improve the community's inclusiveness.

Since most people focus on what to do in building a great community, there are some don'ts as well:

- Don't prioritize growth over demonstrating value to the community.
- Don't forget to educate. Web3, the metaverse and AI are new concepts.
- Don't forget to listen and communicate. The community is a living, breathing group!

Here is one example of an NFT collection that failed to build a strong community and showcase its value.

Porsche entered the NFT market with a 7,500-piece collection of digital images of the 911 Carrera sports car. However, the collection was not well received, with only 16% of the collection being purchased within the first four hours of the mint opening. The following day, only 25% of the collection was sold, leading Porsche to close its mint.

Porsche made three key mistakes in their NFT drop: lack of utility, mistaking audience for community, and a disjointed value proposition.

Porsche failed to provide a clear use case for the collection, and the customizable digital image alone was not enough to instill value for collectors.

Additionally, Porsche did not properly consider community, as they hastily tried to build a Web3 presence with no prior community development. Porsche did not properly educate its user base on NFT ownership, which requires a crypto wallet and a level of Web3 onboarding.

Finally, Porsche struggled to effectively communicate its collection's purpose, making it difficult for customers to understand its value proposition.

These errors highlight the importance of considering utility, community building, and effective communication when launching an NFT collection.

Worksheet: Building a Community with Customer Obsession for Web3 and the Metaverse

1. **Choose the right platform:** Consider the goals and mission of your community, then choose the tools that align with them. Popular platforms include Twitter, Discord, and Telegram.

2. **Understand the Web3, the metaverse and AI ethos:** Get to know the unique culture of the Web3 and metaverse world. Learn the language, join communities, and get to know what makes them tick.

3. **Collaborate with established brands:** Traditional Web2 brands that collaborate with established Web3 and metaverse brands tend to be more successful in entering the space.

4. **Define a clear mission and purpose:** Develop a strategy for your brand's Web3 and metaverse community, including goals, tactics, and metrics for success.

5. **Foster meaningful relationships:** Encourage collaboration and sharing of thoughts through dedicated channels like town hall meetings or weekly Twitter Spaces.

6. **Make it easy for members to contribute:** Give power back to the people and let them know that their contributions matter.

7. **Provide resources, support, and incentives:** Share resources, support, and offer incentives and rewards to encourage participation and engagement.

8. **Encourage diversity and inclusiveness:** Ensure that the community is diverse in thoughts and actions and that diverse backgrounds are represented in leadership and decision-making roles. Continuously gather feedback and improve inclusiveness.

Build World-Class Metaverse Experiences

As this fable showed, to build a successful metaverse strategy, it is important to truly experience what the metaverse is and learn about the potential benefits. It is estimated to grow into an $800B industry by 2024.

The use cases showed that companies can add value to their users by creating immersive marketing opportunities, expanded audience engagement, and new educational opportunities. They can even use the metaverse inside the company as well.

A metaverse strategy can also tap into the growing experience economy, where consumers are more interested in seeking experiences than material possessions. To get started, the approach would be as follows:

1. **Host an immersive education session with your rabbit team.** Hosting an immersive education session with your rabbit team is the first step in exploring the potential of metaverses. This session will provide your team with a comprehensive understanding of the metaverse and its impact on various industries. Team members will learn how to use this new technology to enhance their skills and knowledge. This session will also provide a platform for team members to share their ideas and insights, allowing them to collaborate and gain a deeper understanding of the metaverse.

2. **Play with different metaverses and learn from a variety of use cases.** To maximize the benefits of metaverses, it is essential to play with different metaverses and learn from a variety of use cases. This will provide your team with a diverse perspective on the potential of metaverses and how it can be leveraged to achieve your business goals. Your team can explore the different metaverses and understand their strengths and weaknesses. This exploration will provide valuable insights into

the opportunities and challenges that come with using metaverses.

3. **Determine your business goals.** Your goals can range from internally focused initiatives to customer and partner-focused strategies. It is important to understand the challenges that the metaverse presents for your organization and use a decision framework to navigate it responsibly and strategically. Don't forget to prioritize your goals, assess the impact of metaverses on your organization, and develop a comprehensive plan for success.

4. **Brainstorm!** Brainstorming is a crucial step in taking advantage of the metaverse and planning for its long-term implications and business opportunities. This process involves exploring and discussing potential applications of the metaverse within your organization. You and your team should consider the different ways that metaverses can be leveraged to achieve your business goals, improve processes, and increase efficiency. This stage is also the time to identify potential challenges and limitations that may arise with the integration of metaverses into your organization.

5. **Define a clear vision and goals.** Defining a clear vision and goals for your metaverse strategy is critical to its success. This stage involves aligning your metaverse strategy with your overall business strategy and values. It is important to consider the impact that metaverses will have on your organization and develop goals that are in line with your overall mission and values. This will help ensure that your metaverse strategy is not only effective, but also aligned with your organization's culture and priorities.

6. **Think about the responsible metaverse goals.** When planning for the metaverse, it is essential to consider responsible metaverse goals, including privacy, security, safety, and trust. The metaverse presents unique challenges in these areas, and it

is crucial to ensure that appropriate measures are in place to protect users and their data. This requires a thorough understanding of the potential risks and the measures necessary to mitigate them. By prioritizing privacy, security, safety, and trust in your metaverse strategy, you can build a responsible and sustainable metaverse that supports the long-term success of your organization.

7. **Select a metaverse platform.** Selecting the right metaverse platform is a crucial decision that can impact the success of your metaverse strategy. When considering potential platforms, it is important to align your choice with your vision, goals, and business needs. Factors such as user experience, scalability, and interoperability are important to consider, but privacy by design and default, the risks and rewards of tokenization, digital safety, sustainability, and inclusion and identity should also be considered. This will ensure that the platform you choose supports the long-term success of your metaverse strategy.

8. **Develop user personas.** Developing user personas is an important step in better understanding the needs and behaviors of your target audience in the metaverse. User personas are fictional representations of your ideal users, based on data and insights about their behaviors, motivations, and goals. By developing user personas, you can gain a deeper understanding of the needs and preferences of your target audience, which will help you design an effective user experience in the metaverse.

9. **Design a user experience.** Designing a user experience that aligns with the needs and behaviors of your target audience is critical to the success of your metaverse strategy. That goes for whether it is an internal or external use case. Also remember to think through ease of use, accessibility, and personalization when developing your user experience. The metaverse provides a unique opportunity to create a personalized and immersive experience for your users, and a great user experience can help increase engagement and loyalty. By considering the needs

and behaviors of your target audience, you can create a user experience that is both effective and enjoyable, helping to drive the success of your metaverse strategy.

10. **Create content for the metaverse.** Content creation is a key aspect of your metaverse strategy. To effectively leverage the metaverse, you will need to create digital assets, environments, and experiences that align with your vision and goals. This includes designing virtual environments that engage and immerse users and creating digital assets such as avatars, objects, and interactive experiences. It is important to consider the unique opportunities and limitations of the metaverse when creating content and to focus on creating experiences that are both memorable and impactful.

11. **Create a handbook.** A handbook for responsible innovation and use of the metaverse can help ensure that your organization is operating in a manner that aligns with your values and goals. This handbook should outline principles and guidance for the responsible use of the metaverse, including considerations around privacy, security, safety, and trust. It should also provide guidance on how to navigate the unique challenges and opportunities presented by the metaverse, ensuring that your organization is able to leverage this new technology in a responsible and sustainable manner.

12. **Build a strong and engaged community.** Building a strong and engaged community in the metaverse is critical to the success of your metaverse strategy. Providing opportunities for members to connect, collaborate, and engage with your brand will help to increase engagement and loyalty and will also provide valuable insights into the needs and behaviors of your target audience. This can include hosting virtual events, facilitating discussions and collaboration, and providing opportunities for members to engage with your brand through virtual experiences. By building a strong community, you can create a vibrant and engaging metaverse that supports the long-term

success of your organization. (See the Community Is the Project section.)

13. **Develop a monetization strategy.** Developing a monetization strategy that aligns with your vision, goals, and community is a critical aspect of your metaverse strategy. There are several options for monetizing your metaverse presence, including in-world transactions, advertising, and subscriptions. It is important to consider factors such as the needs and behaviors of your target audience as well as market trends and best practices when developing your monetization strategy. By aligning your monetization strategy with your vision and goals, you can ensure that it supports the long-term success of your metaverse strategy.

14. **Establish metrics and KPIs.** Establishing metrics and KPIs to measure the success of your metaverse strategy is essential to ensuring that it stays on track and delivers results. Key metrics to track include user engagement, revenue, and community growth. These metrics will help you understand the effectiveness of your metaverse strategy and will provide valuable insights into areas for improvement. By regularly tracking and analyzing these metrics, you can ensure that your metaverse strategy is delivering results and supporting the long-term success of your organization.

15. **Continually optimize.** Continual optimization of your metaverse strategy is critical to ensuring that it stays relevant and competitive over time. Market trends, user feedback, and performance metrics are key sources of information that can help inform your optimization efforts. Regularly reviewing and refining your metaverse strategy in light of these factors will help ensure that it stays aligned with your vision and goals and that it continues to deliver results over the long term. By taking a data-driven and iterative approach to optimization, you can ensure that your metaverse strategy stays competitive and relevant in a rapidly evolving market.

This framework is a starting point and may need to be adapted or expanded based on your specific business needs and the rapidly evolving metaverse market.

Worksheet: Metaverse

   I. Host an Immersive Education Session
      1. Purpose: To provide a comprehensive understanding of the metaverse and its impact on various industries.
      2. Outcome: Increased knowledge and skills on metaverse technology, collaborative insights, and ideas shared among team members.
  II. Play with Different Metaverses
      1. Purpose: To maximize benefits of metaverses and learn from a variety of use cases.
      2. Outcome: Diverse perspective on potential of metaverses, valuable insights into opportunities and challenges.
 III. Determine Business Goals
      1. Purpose: To align metaverse strategy with overall business strategy and values.
      2. Outcome: Prioritized goals, assessment of metaverse impact on organization, comprehensive plan for success.
 IV. Brainstorm
      1. Purpose: To explore and discuss potential applications of the metaverse within the organization.
      2. Outcome: Potential applications and challenges identified, deeper understanding of metaverse integration into organization.
  V. Define Clear Vision and Goals
      1. Purpose: To align metaverse strategy with overall business strategy and values.
      2. Outcome: Aligned metaverse strategy with mission and values, effective and culturally aligned strategy.

VI. Think About Responsible Metaverse Goals

　1. Purpose: To ensure appropriate measures are in place to protect users and their data.

　2. Outcome: Prioritized privacy, security, safety, and trust; responsible and sustainable metaverse strategy.

VII. Select Metaverse Platform

　1. Purpose: To choose a platform that aligns with vision, goals, and business needs.

　2. Outcome: Platform selected supports long-term success of metaverse strategy.

VIII. Develop User Personas

　1. Purpose: To better understand the needs and behaviors of target audience in the metaverse.

　2. Outcome: Deeper understanding of target audience needs and preferences.

IX. Design User Experience

　1. Purpose: To design a user experience that aligns with target audience needs and behaviors.

　2. Outcome: Effective and enjoyable user experience, increased engagement and loyalty.

X. Create Content for the Metaverse

　1. Purpose: To create digital assets, environments, and experiences that align with vision and goals.

　2. Outcome: Memorable and impactful virtual environments and digital assets.

XI. Create Handbook

　1. Purpose: To ensure responsible innovation and use of the metaverse.

　2. Outcome: Principles and guidance for responsible use of the metaverse outlined; responsible use of the metaverse ensured.

Don't Forget to Augment Your Intelligence with AI

We all know what AI is: human intelligence in machines that are designed to think and act like humans. AI systems can be trained to perform tasks such as pattern recognition, decision-making, and language understanding.

But the term augmented intelligence is much more appropriate. AI is a tool, but it's like having a partner on your project. And as far as partners go, they are dependable and hard-working but require guidance, direction, correction, and care. However, despite their shortcomings, having AI as a partner will let you do more, faster, and better.

The use of AI Tools as a copilot to your company in developing your strategy enables you to go further. For example, you can use ChatGPT to create your KPIs, but as a change agent in a brand-new space, you have to add in context, common sense, and business knowledge.

AI will help us work differently. Learn to use AI as tools for coding, writing, creating music, art, and more. For example, AI can play a significant role in the metaverse by creating digital avatars and characters that can interact with users in real time. These avatars can be designed to have their own personalities, behaviors, and responses, providing a more immersive and interactive experience for users. AI can even help you generate an NFT collection. Brian Fanzo, of NFT365, is creating and selling a one-of-a-kind art piece every day this year.

The relationship between AI, Web3, and the metaverse can be seen as complementary, with each having the potential to enhance the other. AI can provide the metaverse with more sophisticated and lifelike digital entities, while Web3 can provide a decentralized and secure infrastructure for the metaverse.

Following are ways that your company could leverage and use AI to make your strategy more powerful.

- **Web3 and metaverse marketing.** One of the best use cases for AI in Web3 and metaverse marketing is as a conversational AI for chatbots. With its advanced language understanding capabilities, ChatGPT can be integrated into chatbots to provide users with human-like responses and assist them with tasks such as answering questions, guiding them through a process, or helping them make a purchase. This can be particularly useful for decentralized applications (dApps) and other Web3 services that require a high level of user engagement and support. By providing a conversational interface, ChatGPT can help dApps and Web3 services improve user experience, increase user engagement, and streamline customer support operations.

- **Content creation.** AI can help with content creation by automating certain tasks and providing new opportunities for content creation. For example, AI language models such as ChatGPT can generate text and content that are similar to that written by humans. This can save time and effort compared to manual content creation and also provide new and creative perspectives for content creation.

AI can be helpful generating content for Web3 and the metaverse, such as generating tutorials and explainer articles. AI can be used to generate comprehensive and easy-to-understand articles that explain complex Web3 and metaverse concepts to users. These articles can help educate users about the benefits of decentralized technology and how they can use and interact with Web3 services and the metaverse.

Another example is in creating engaging social media posts. AI can be used to generate social media posts that promote Web3 services and the metaverse. These posts can be designed to be engaging, informative, and shareable, helping to raise awareness and drive engagement with these technologies.

And a final example is in writing compelling virtual world narratives. AI can be used to write compelling narratives that can be used to build and develop virtual worlds within the metaverse. These narratives can be used to create rich and immersive experiences for users and to drive engagement with avatars and characters within the metaverse.

- **Avatars and NFT collections.** AI has the potential to significantly impact the art world by enabling the creation of new forms of digital art and by enabling artists to create more sophisticated and interactive works.

Several AI tools can be used to generate non-fungible tokens (NFTs) and avatars. Here are a few popular ones:

- DALL-E: A state-of-the-art deep learning AI model developed by OpenAI that creates highly detailed images from textual descriptions
- GPT-3: Another OpenAI language model that can be used to generate NFTs and avatars by converting text into images
- MakeHuman: An open-source software for generating 3D human models for animation, games, and more
- DAZ Studio: A free 3D art creation software that allows users to generate highly detailed human avatars for use in various digital media
- Artbreeder: A generative art platform that uses AI to combine existing images and generate new, unique images that can be used as NFTs

These are just a few examples, and many other tools are available that can be used to generate NFTs and avatars using AI.

AI algorithms can be trained on existing art styles and used to generate new and original pieces of art. These AI-generated artworks can then be transformed into NFTs and traded in the metaverse. In addition, you can create unique and sophisticated avatars that can be used as characters in virtual worlds within the metaverse. They can be designed to have their own personalities, behaviors, and responses and can interact with users in real time.

You can also create immersive and interactive experiences within the metaverse, such as virtual exhibitions, galleries, and interactive installations.

- **Podcasts.** AI can be used in podcasts for Web3 and the metaverse. AI-powered virtual hosts can be used to host podcasts within the metaverse. These hosts can interact with listeners, answer questions, and provide a more immersive and engaging experience.

  The tools can also be used to provide personalized experiences for listeners within the metaverse, such as recommending episodes or virtual events based on their interests. Imagine AI recommending the right set of education for Web3 or new users. And the tools can be used to enhance the audio quality of podcasts within the metaverse, such as removing background noise and optimizing sound levels.

- **Virtual metaverse tour guides.** It is projected that by 2026, a quarter of the global population will be daily metaverse users. This presents an exciting opportunity for businesses to create innovative AI-powered virtual tour guides that can effectively introduce users to each new metaverse they visit. What will these AI-tour guides do? AI can help first-time users get a thorough introduction to the metaverse and ensure that tech-savvy users have a seamless experience. AI could be a way to create an exceptional user experience.

- **Industrial metaverses. It is projected that in six years, digital twins used as industrial metaverses will make the need for physical testing obsolete.** The use of digital twins within the industrial metaverse can have significant benefits for manufacturers, including increased efficiency, reduced downtime, and improved product quality. By using digital twins, manufacturers can simulate and test products and processes virtually, reducing the need for physical prototypes and tests. This can lead to cost savings, faster time-to-market, and more sustainable production practices. Overall, the industrial metaverse and digital twins represent a powerful combination of technology that can revolutionize the way products are designed, manufactured, and maintained.

Worksheet: AI Tools for Web3 and Metaverse

1. Customer Experience
   - Personalization and recommendations for in-world content and experiences
   - Chatbots for customer support and engagement
   - Predictive analytics for customer behavior and preferences
2. Content Creation and Management
   - Automated asset generation and optimization
   - Content moderation and filtering
   - Analytics and insights for content performance and optimization
3. Virtual Event and Experience Management
   - Virtual event creation and management, including audience management and analytics
   - Virtual experience creation and optimization, including environment design and user experience
   - Predictive analytics for virtual event and experience performance and optimization
4. Virtual Economy and Commerce
   - Virtual goods and services marketplace creation and management
   - Pricing and inventory management for virtual goods and services
   - Fraud detection and prevention for virtual transactions

5. Community Management
   - User behavior monitoring and moderation
   - Community engagement and growth strategies
   - Analytics for community health and growth
6. Data Management and Insights
   - Data collection, analysis, and visualization for user behavior and preferences
   - Predictive analytics for business performance and optimization
   - Integration with data analytics and business intelligence tools
7. Security and Compliance
   - Authentication and authorization management for users and transactions
   - Data privacy and security management
   - Compliance with legal and regulatory requirements for virtual transactions and environments
8. Digital Twins for Industrial Metaverses
   - Efficiency in testing products and prototypes
   - Reduced downtime through testing processes in a virtual world
   - Increased product quality in manufacturing

The Business Case

The final step is to build a business case for your execution and experiments.

Because we are early in the space, consider investing in tech with multiple uses in the Web3, the metaverse and AI to have both near- and long-term benefits. Start with enhancing the existing brand presence, being mindful of data security and privacy and having smart pricing strategies for virtual goods and services.

The goal is to meet both business needs and consumer desires in Web3, the metaverse and AI, making sure to build consistency among digital presences and reinforce brand voice. The metaverse provides a unique opportunity to engage customers, build brand, and strengthen workforce experience in a new immersive digital world.

A top question that is asked is around revenue streams.

Revenue streams for Web3 digital identity could come in the form of rewards that you build into your profile. Web3 technologies can help drive revenue by attracting and retaining customers through loyalty programs. By offering loyalty points and rewards based on NFTs that can be redeemed in real time and provide a unique and immersive experience, businesses can incentivize customers to spend more on their products and services.

Additionally, by expanding reward options and offering digital collectibles and cryptocurrencies, businesses can attract a younger audience, increase customer engagement, and improve user experience, leading to increased customer loyalty and repeat purchases. Overall, Web3 loyalty programs have the potential to drive revenue by creating a more loyal customer base and increasing sales.

Potential revenue streams for the metaverse include virtual goods and experiences, advertising, subscriptions, user fees, data and insights, licensing and royalties, and strategic partnerships.

Virtual goods and experiences include sales of virtual real estate, digital clothing and accessories, and unique experiences such as attending virtual concerts or events. Advertisers could pay for virtual billboards, sponsorships, and other forms of in-world advertising, providing a new and immersive platform for advertisers to reach consumers. Subscriptions could be charged for access to premium content, experiences, or services within the metaverse, while user fees could be charged for activities such as creating and hosting virtual events or for buying and selling virtual goods and services.

Worksheet: Business Case for Web3, the metaverse and AI

Market Assessment

Estimate the size of the metaverse market and its growth potential

- Consider factors such as user adoption, demographic trends, and technology advancements.
- Analyze the competitive landscape.
- Identify key players in the metaverse market.
- Understand opportunities and challenges in the market.
- Determine how your company can differentiate itself from others.

Revenue Streams

- Virtual goods and experiences
  - Sales of virtual real estate, digital clothing and accessories, and unique experiences.
- Reward programs
  - Building loyalty programs based on NFTs can help attract new users.
- Advertising
  - Virtual billboards, sponsorships, and other forms of in-world advertising.
- Subscriptions
  - Access to premium content, experiences, or services within the metaverse.
- User fees
  - Activities such as creating and hosting virtual events, buying and selling virtual goods and services.

- Licensing and royalties
  - Licensing of technology, content, and intellectual property to other companies.
- Strategic partnerships
  - Co-creation and co-marketing of metaverse experiences with other companies.

Technology and Infrastructure

- Assess the technology and infrastructure requirements for building and operating a metaverse.
- Hardware, software, and network capacity.

Legal and Regulatory Considerations

- Consider legal and regulatory considerations associated with building a metaverse.
- Intellectual property rights, data privacy, and consumer protection laws.

Business Model

- Develop a business model that outlines how the metaverse will generate revenue and create value for users, shareholders, and stakeholders.

Investment Costs and Funding

- Estimate investment costs associated with building and operating the metaverse.
- Potential sources of funding, such as venture capital, strategic partnerships, and public offerings.

Conclusion

This model of the five emPOWERments is a starting point for your organization. Reinvent it and customize it as you go. Consider it guidance for working in Web3 and the metaverse and how AI tooling can help. It serves as an approach and critical elements to think through. Given the Web3, AI, and metaverse space is in such an early state, it is about questions to ask your company, elements to define for a business case, ways to start a branding approach, and how to focus on community. But just as EdgyMaven must adjust and learn through experimentation, so must you.

Share freely those experiences so we all can learn together. That is, after all, the ethos of Web3, the metaverse and AI.

A
Glossary

A

airdrop A marketing technique in which crypto projects send their native tokens directly to the wallets of their users to increase awareness and adoption.

altcoin Any cryptocurrency that wasn't Bitcoin; any new cryptocurrency with a relatively small market cap.

avatar A digital representation of a person for use in a game, metaverse, or digital universe.

B

Bitcoin The very first decentralized, peer-to-peer, digital currency, created by the pseudonymous Satoshi Nakamoto in 2009.

blockchain A publicly accessible digital ledger used to store and transfer information without the need for a central authority. Blockchains are the core technology on which cryptocurrency protocols like Bitcoin and Ethereum are built.

blockchain domain An easy-to-remember address for sending and receiving crypto. Instead of having to copy and paste long, complicated crypto addresses like bc1qw508d6qejxtdg4y5r3zarvary0c5xw7kv8-f3t4, you can simply type in a blockchain domain like sandy.domain. Names minted on the blockchain allow people to govern their

207

own data, set their Web3 username, take control of their digital worlds, and harness the power of the internet.

C

cryptocurrency   A digital asset designed to be used as a medium of exchange. Cryptocurrencies are borderless, secure, and maintained by blockchains as opposed to centralized banks or governments.

D

DAO   *See* decentralized autonomous organization.

Dapp   *See* decentralized application.

decentralization   The transfer of control and decision-making from a centralized entity (individual, organization, or group thereof) to a distributed network. Decentralized networks strive to reduce the level of trust that participants must place in one another and stop their ability to exert authority or control over one another in ways that degrade the functionality of the network.

decentralized application (Dapp)   An application built on open-source code that lives on the blockchain. Dapps exist independent of centralized groups or figures and often incentivize users to maintain them through rewarded tokens.

decentralized autonomous organization (DAO)   An organization based on open-source code and governed by its users. DAOs typically focus on a specific project or mission and trade the traditional hierarchical systems of legacy corporations for guidelines written on the blockchain.

decentralized finance (DeFi)   The ecosystem of borderless, trustless, peer-to-peer financial tools being built on public blockchains without the use of banks. DeFi apps are built to be open and interconnected, allowing them to be used in conjunction with one another.

DeFi   *See* decentralized finance.

digital identity   The body of information about an individual, organization, or entity that exists online. This digital identity is owned by each person, entity, or company and stores data about them. Web3 is seen as potentially bridging the gap between an individual's physical identity and their digital identity via blockchain technology. This suggests that everyone will have a "digital identity," which encompasses both their online and real-world legal versions. *See also* Web3.

E

Ethereum A public blockchain serving as the foundation for decentralized applications. *See also* decentralized application (Dapp).
exchange A business that allows customers to trade crypto or digital currencies.

F

fiat A currency established as legal tender, such as the US dollar, often backed and regulated by a government.

G

gas A fee paid by a user to conduct a transaction or execute a smart contract on the Ethereum blockchain.
gm A greeting. gm stands for "good morning," but in the Web3 and metaverse world, it is more than a greeting because it expresses that idea that "we are early" and our future is bright.

L

L1 *See* layer 1 (L1).
L2 *See* layer 2 (L2).
layer 1 (L1) The first layer of the Open Systems Interconnection (OSI) model. It is the actual components that process and transmit digital data. It is commonly known at the blockchain platform itself, like Bitcoin or Ethereum.
layer 2 (L2) Layer 2 refers to the second layer of the Open Systems Interconnection (OSI) model, which is the data link layer. Layer 2 is where data packets are encoded and decoded into actual bits.

Unlike sidechains, which use their own consensus mechanisms, layer 2 solutions are secured by their underlying mainchain.

M

metaverse   A 3D digital world where people work, play, and sleep. The experience melds the physical and virtual worlds in a way that feels real and permanent. *The simplest definition is the internet in 3D.*

minting   The process of validating information, such as domain ownership, and registering that onto the blockchain.

N

NFT   *See non-fungible token.*

noncustodial   The private keys and seed phrase for a user's wallet are stored locally on the user's device and not on any centralized server. This enhances security and puts users in full control of their funds.

non-fungible token (NFT)   A digital asset based on blockchain technology. Anything can become an NFT—a piece of art, sports memorabilia, music, and more.

O

OMA3   *See* Open Metaverse Alliance (OMA3).

OpenID   An open standard and decentralized authentication protocol promoted by the nonprofit OpenID Foundation. OpenID allows you to use an existing account to sign into multiple websites, without needing to create new passwords.

Open Metaverse Alliance (OMA3)   A consortium of the leading Web3 and metaverse firms that have come together to solve the industry's interoperability issues. In a nutshell, OMA3 aims to create uniform standards and ease access across all Web3 and metaverse platforms.

R

Roblox   A massively multiplayer online game platform that allows users to create their own games and play games created by other users. It's designed to be accessible to players of all ages.

Robux   A premium currency within the world of Roblox that you can use to buy new games, private servers, and some other goodies.

S

smart contract   A self-executing contract—meaning that the terms of the agreement between buyer and seller are directly written into lines of code. Smart contracts are based on blockchain technology and are stored and replicated on a blockchain network.

stablecoin   A token backed by a fiat currency, like the US dollar, or pegged to physical assets like precious metals or even other cryptocurrencies like Bitcoin.

T

trustless   A system that does not rely on any central authority or intermediary to function. The system can function and be trusted without the need for any specific person or organization to oversee or control it. Instead, trust is placed in the code and the network, which are transparent and tamperproof.

W

wallet   A software application or hardware device used to store the private keys to blockchain assets and accounts. Examples include Coinbase Wallet, Ledger, MetaMask, and Trust Wallet.

Web3   An open movement to broadly decentralize the internet, allowing for individual ownership of identity and personal data.

B

Additional Thoughts on DAOs

To DAO or Not to DAO: That Is the Question

Traditional focus groups can be time-consuming and costly, and the results may not be representative of actual user experiences because participants are paid and may not be as invested in the product as real users. However, if a company already has an active user base, it can leverage this by giving users the ability to form a DAO. This allows the community to vote on new product ideas and provide feedback throughout the entire innovation and selling process. By doing this, companies can gather feedback from an enthusiastic user base and test products across the entire life cycle before launch.

DAOs as the New Membership Club

Social clubs and subscription-based business models have a long history, and now, with the advent of NFTs, these models can be synced with product manufacturing to create a new type of membership club. By linking a monthly product subscription to a membership, NFT holders can create a treasury, vote on products they want, and even hold their membership as a digital asset until they want to resell it. This new model offers a unique way to bring together a community and sustain operations through NFT sales and creator fees.

Steps to Building a DAO

Following are the suggested steps to build a DAO:

1. **Outline a clear mission.** Choose a name that is implicitly tied to the mission. The mission should be easily understandable and should bring together a community.

2. **Decide on ownership.** Determine the voting system, such as allocating one vote per person or per token, to avoid the possibility of being controlled by a single entity. Ownership decisions are made by the members who hold tokens that give them voting rights. These decisions can range from electing board members, choosing the direction of the organization, and determining the allocation of funds. It's important for DAO members to carefully consider their ownership decisions as they will directly impact the success and stability of the organization. These decisions should be based on a clear understanding of the organization's goals and a thorough evaluation of the options available. Additionally, members should consider the long-term consequences of their decisions and ensure that they align with the overall mission of the DAO. By making informed ownership decisions, members can help to ensure the continued growth and success of the DAO.

3. **Fund the DAO.** DAOs are typically funded through a combination of initial coin offerings (ICOs), token sales, and ongoing revenue streams. In an ICO, a new cryptocurrency is created and sold to investors in exchange for ether, the native cryptocurrency of the Ethereum blockchain. These funds can be used to cover the initial development costs of the DAO and to incentivize early adopters.

After the ICO, DAOs can continue to generate revenue through various means, such as charging transaction fees on their decentralized applications (dapps), collecting a percentage of profits from projects that the DAO invests in, or through recurring subscription-based revenue streams. The funds generated by these revenue streams can then be used to support ongoing development and maintenance of the DAO as well as to reward participants for their contributions. Remember our case study on the PizzaDAO. They used the funds from the NFT sale and ongoing creator fees from the resale to sustain operations.

4. **Decide on a proposal system.** Choose from a variety of proposal systems to manage the governance process. Some popular proposal systems include governance through token voting, Aragon Governance, DAOstack, and Colony. In token voting, token holders cast votes on proposals using their tokens, which is a widely used method in DeFi protocols and blockchain projects. Aragon Governance is a platform built on Ethereum that allows DAOs to create and manage their own governance process, including proposals and voting. DAOstack is a modular platform that enables DAOs to create and manage proposals, voting, and other governance processes in a scalable and user-friendly way. Colony is a platform for decentralized organizations that enables members to propose and vote on decisions, allocate funds, and manage tasks and projects. The best proposal system for a DAO depends on its specific needs and goals. This could be a quorum for different levels of financial outlays.

5. **Foster communication.** This enables people to contribute and make decisions collectively. Utilizing transparent platforms, such as a public forum or a blockchain-based platform, can ensure that all members have equal access to information and can participate in discussions. For instance, many DAOs use

Discord. In addition, regular updates, such as newsletters or progress reports, can help keep all members informed about the status of the DAO and its activities. And finally in-person or virtual meetings, such as town hall sessions or video conferences, can provide an opportunity for members to voice their concerns and ask questions. These communications can all drive a sense of community among members and help build trust. By using a combination of these communication methods, a DAO can ensure that all members are well informed, engaged, and involved in the decision-making process.

About the Author

Sandy Carter is a leading voice in technology, social media, and Web3, the metaverse and AI who has been recognized as top 10 most powerful women in tech per CNN. She is currently chief operating officer and head of business development at Unstoppable Domains as well as the founder of Unstoppable Women of Web3.

As chief operating officer, she is responsible for creating business strategies, driving growth, and moving the company's long-term goals forward. In this role, she is responsible for driving new partnerships and integrations for Web 3.0 and the metaverse. Her mission is to onboard the world onto the decentralized web by building blockchain-based identity platforms. Her previous role was at Amazon Web Services, where she was a vice president, creating and growing businesses through AI, IoT, Cloud and emerging technologies. She was also a general manager at IBM focused on AI and IoT and a Silicon Valley start-up founder.

Sandy is also board member at Altair, chairman of the board for the nonprofit organization Girls in Tech, a member of Diversity Community at the World Economic Forum, and the founder of Unstoppable Women of Web3 as well as a founding member of Blockchain Friends Forever (BFF) and 1000 Faces, a global NFT project. She joined the first ringing of the bell on the NASDAQ in the metaverse. She has won numerous awards, including Top 100 Global Thought Leader by *Awards* magazine, Top 150 Business Transformational Leaders, a Top 100 Chief Tech Leader, Top 115 Most Inspirational Women of Web3/Metaverse, 100 Women Davos, Two Lovies Awards for Best Metaverse HQ, Top 14 Edge Leader, Federal 100 Award Winner, CRN Channel Chief, and a member of *Fortune*'s Most Powerful Women.

She is fluent in eight programming languages and is the author of five books:

- *Extreme Innovation* (2017)
- *Geek Girls Are Chic* (2015)
- *Get Bold* (2011)
- *The New Language of Business* (2010)
- *The New Language of Marketing* (2008)

She has won the Platinum MarCom Award and the Silver Marketing Sherpa award.

Sandy is the proud mother of two daughters.

AFTERWORD

Matt Gould, CEO and Founder of Unstoppable Domains

Sandy joined Unstoppable on our path to becoming a unicorn because she was excited about delivering digital identity for the world and the impact that could have on our joint digital experiences. Sandy has fielded many questions about Web3 and the metaverse, spoken at numerous Web3 events, and started several leading industry groups to educate more people, especially women and diverse groups about the potential of Web3. Sandy's desire to share her learnings and experiences in a fun way comes through in this wonderful tale.

In *The Tiger and the Rabbit,* Sandy Carter introduces us to a compelling story about the transformation of a struggling company called EdgyMaven. Through the eyes of Victoria McSay, the chief growth officer, we see how a diverse team of experts comes together to explore the potential of Web3, AI, and the metaverse to solve real-world problems around customer experience and engagement. As we follow their journey, we witness the power of decentralized technology, community, and inclusivity to unleash a new era of innovation and creativity.

As someone who has been involved in the Web3, metaverse and AI for many years, I can tell you that Sandy Carter is uniquely qualified to write this book. Her deep understanding of the communities and business of blockchain and decentralized applications has helped countless companies and individuals navigate the complex landscape of Web3. She has been a tireless advocate for community-driven innovation and has worked with some of the most visionary entrepreneurs and developers in the industry. Her experience and insights are invaluable to anyone who wants to understand the potential of Web3 and the metaverse.

Throughout the book, Sandy introduces us to a diverse cast of characters who represent different backgrounds and skills. From Dawn Alek, an experienced educator, to Tommy Seaport, a skilled gamer, to Greg Dashed, a technology pioneer, each team member brings unique perspectives and expertise to the table. Together, they explore the challenges and opportunities of Web3, AI, and the metaverse, and discover new ways to engage with customers and create value.

One of the key takeaways from this book is the importance of experimentation and exploration. As Sandy and her team show us, the world of Web3, AI, and the metaverse is still in its early stages, and there is much to learn and discover. By taking a bold and open-minded approach, we can uncover new possibilities and create solutions that were once unthinkable.

As someone who has had the privilege of working with Sandy, I can attest to her passion, dedication, and expertise. She has been an inspiration to me and many others in the Web3 community, and I'm confident that her book will be a valuable resource for anyone who wants to explore the future of digital innovation with their teams.

So, whether you're a seasoned entrepreneur, a curious investor, or a passionate technologist, *The Tiger and the Rabbit: A Fable of Harnessing the Power of the Metaverse, Web3, and AI for Business Success* is a must-read. It's a fascinating story about the power of technology to transform our lives, our communities, and our world. I hope you enjoy it as much as I did.

Index